# THE MEDIA LAW DICTIONARY

## John Murray
Michigan State University

UNIVERSITY
PRESS OF
AMERICA

LANHAM • NEW YORK • LONDON

# PREFACE

This book grows out of 13 years experience in teaching majors in mass media disciplines at undergraduate and graduate levels the in's and out's of freedom of expression under the First Amendment, or trying at least to teach them. This vocabulary book will, I believe, be helpful to future students and to present practitioners in the world of mass media. Its purpose is to bring together words and phrases commonly appearing in media law. Many of the terms are standard law terms, others have acquired artful meanings within mass media decisions and are not readily available to non-lawyers, requiring as they do a context to give them meaning. Casual browsing through the pages will illustrate how such terms are tied to mass media and the First Amendment wherever possible. No claim is made that this dictionary is all-inclusive, but I believe it is sufficiently complete to be a valuable adjunct book to mass media courses dealing with law questions and for news handlers and editorialists interested in First Amendment issues. Any errors are, of course, mine.

John Murray
Professor, Journalism
Michigan State University

# table of contents

# a

**Absolute Test.** The doctrine that the First Amendment is to be read literally as meaning that government has no power to punish expression, neither the federal government under the First Amendment nor state governments because the First applies to them through the Fourteenth Amendment. U.S. Supreme Court Justices Hugo L. Black and William O. Douglas went farthest along this road in their First Amendment judgments, but the doctrine has never had majority support on the court. Douglas saw expression as punishable only when it was "so closely brigaded with illegal action as to be an inseparable part of it," *Roth v. United States*, and Black saw no right to speak where there was no right to be: "While I have always believed that under the First and Fourteenth Amendments neither the state nor the federal government has any authority to regulate or censor the content of speech, I have never believed that any person has a right to give speeches or engage in demonstrations where he pleases and when he pleases." *Tinker v. Des Moines Independent School District*.

**Abstention Doctrine.** Federal courts will avoid deciding a case on constitutional grounds if the case can be reached on some other basis, i.e., the constitutional question is reached only if other grounds to affirm or reverse are not present. The doctrine is illustrated in a case involving access to police records in St. Louis. The federal district court abstained from deciding the case because concurrent cases in state courts might be decided in a way that would avoid the federal constitutional questions raised in the case. The U.S. Court of Appeals, Eighth Circuit, chose not to apply the abstention doctrine to one of three issues raised in the original suit because "state court review of the state constitutional issue, which may make our decision of the federal constitutional issues unnecessary, is likely to be significantly delayed." *Herald Co. v. McNeal*.

**Abstractions Test.** A phrase of imprecise meaning sometimes used as a guide in copyright infringement cases. In such a case, Anne Nichols, author of Abie's Irish Rose, a durable hit play, unsuccessfully claimed infringement by a motion picture, The Cohens and the Kelleys. The question was how close must one plot, sequence and characters parallel another's work as to infringe, or how far can one "abstract" from

1

another's work without jeopardy. The court ruled that rights protected by copyright "cannot be limited literally to the text, else a plagiarist would escape by immaterial variations." Therefore, "literal appropriation" was not the test. "But when the plagiarist does not take out a block in situ, but an abstract of the whole, decision is more troublesome." So while the court agreed that "two plays may correspond in plot closely enough for infringement," it found an insufficient abstraction in this instance. For infringement, more would be required than the mere fact of two comedies "based upon conflicts between Irish and Jews, into which the marriage of their children enters . . . ." *Nichols v. Universal Pictures.*

**Access to Information.** "It has generally been held that the First Amendment does not guarantee the press a constitutional right of special access to information not available to the public generally." *Branzburg v. Hayes*, and "...press is regularly excluded from grand jury proceedings, from our own conferences, the meetings of other official bodies gathered in executive session, and the meetings of private organizations. Newsmen have no constitutional right of access to the scenes of crime or disaster when the general public is excluded and they may be prohibited from attending or publishing information about trials if such restrictions are necessary to assure a defendant a fair trial before an impartial tribunal." To be applicable, the "if" clause at the end of that statement would, under prior restraint decisions, require a heavy burden of proof; and, further, the clause should be set beside another doctrine repetitively quoted by courts: "What transpires in the court room is public property....Those who see and hear what transpired may report it with impunity. There is no special perquisite of the judiciary which enables it, as distinguished from other institutions of democratic government, to suppress, edit, or censor events which transpire in proceedings before it." *Craig v. Harney.* Another modification is seen in a case involving access to a prison. The U.S. Court of Appeals, Ninth Circuit, said that public and media rights to visit a prison need not be "implemented identically" because the access needs are different. "Media access, on reasonable notice, may be desirable in the wake of a newsworthy event, while the interest of the public in observing jail conditions may be satisfied by formal, scheduled tours." *KQED, Inc. and NAACP v. Houchins.* In that case, however, the U.S. Supreme Court ruled against allowing cameras and reporters to enter a California jail, using the no "special access" reasoning from *Branzburg (The New York Times, 6/27/78, p. 31).* One of the plurality of four, Justice

Potter Stewart, argued that jail-visiting restrictions on individuals could be "unreasonable as applied to journalists," and three dissenters argued for "some measure of constitutional protection" for gathering news of "public institutions such as prisons."

**Access to Media.** There is no enforceable right of access to the news, editorial or advertising pages of a publication, nor to advertising over licensed media. There is a contingent right of access to broadcast media when political attacks or political editorials are involved, and an ambiguous "right" under the Fairness Doctrine generally. Access to any media as a news outlet depends on the judgment of reporters and editors as to what is news and not on the judgment of the news source.

**Ad Hoc Balancing Test.** It's questionable whether adding "ad hoc" (Latin—meaning for an isolated purpose as in ad hoc committee) creates any significant difference between this term and the "balancing test" itself (weighing other societal needs against the First Amendment on the scales of decision). Chief Justice Fred M. Vinson expressed the sometimes so-called ad hoc approach this way in *American Communications Association v. Douds*, which upheld a federal law denying National Labor Relations Board privileges to any union leader refusing to certify that he had no connection with Communists: "When particular conduct is regulated in the interest of public order, and the regulation results in an indirect, conditional, partial abridgment of speech, the duty of the court is to determine which of these two conflicting interests demands the greater protection under the particular circumstances presented."

**Adjective Law.** The body of rules governing procedures of law by which issues (substantive law) are resolved. Proper procedure is inseparably twined with the substance of law and is critically important in the protection of property and personal rights. The more common term today is procedural law.

**Adjudication.** The determination of matters in dispute by a court or tribunal. It covers both the process and the decision. If referring to the outcome, the phrase "decision of the court" is more understandable to most people than "the adjudication by the court."

3

# a

**Administrative Law Judge.** Persons authorized to conduct hearings for 28 federal agencies. Their authority comes from the Administrative Procedures Act of 1946. Prior to 1973, they were called hearing examiners. Similar titles and functions exist in state governments.

**Administrative Procedure Act.** A federal law (many states have similar ones) of interest to media in that it requires government agencies having quasi-legislative powers (e.g. Federal Communications Commission and Federal Trade Commission) to give the public an opportunity to be heard in the rule-making process. Proposed new rules must be published in the Federal Register and interested persons must be allowed to respond by written comments. Another important aspect of this act is that it requires the agency to hold a formal hearing for a person aggrieved with agency actions.

**Adversary Relationship.** The role of media in relation to government is sometimes described as adversary in that one function of media is to watchdog against misconduct or unnecessary secrecy in government. Another media function implied in the metaphor is to question adversely government officials on programs and policies. The metaphor comes from law, but the comparison limps. The adversary system applies to American courts and means that legal proceedings are a forum of contestants governed by agreed on rules of evidence before an impartial judge. Further, the adversary system presumes innocence. The other system of trials is the accusatory system, used in continental law, wherein the accused must disprove the accusation.

**Advertising Agent.** The American Association of Advertising Agencies says the term is "merely a trade name commonly used to designate a concern engaged in rendering advertising service. The name is a misnomer and a senseless survivor from the days when it meant a broker of space." The word "agent" or "agency" in law, however, has a specific meaning. "Agency" is a relationship of trust and responsibility (a fiduciary relationship) which comes about when one person consents that another shall act on his behalf and under his control and the second person consents so to act.

**Advertising—Fairness Doctrine.** The Federal Communications Commission exempts from the Fairness Doctrine product commercials which do not "obviously and meaningfully address a controversial issue of public importance," and the policy was upheld by the U.S. Court of Appeals, District of Columbia Circuit, in *National Citizens*

*Committee for Broadcasting v. FCC*. The court reasoned that "merely advocating the use of a product" does not of itself raise a controversial issue, even if the product is controversial in the minds of some viewers. Against the argument that commercial speech is under the First Amendment and therefore product advertising should trigger the Fairness Doctrine, the court said that ". . . not all speech which contributes meaningfully to public debate" must be subject to the fairness concept. "There is an obvious difference between the standard employed . . . for determining whether the fairness doctrine applies to advertisements—that is, whether the advertisement advocates one side of a controversial public issue—and the holding . . . that advertising is protected by the first amendment because it represents dissemination of valuable information important to the functioning of a free enterprise system. Nothing in the Supreme Court's decision . . . upholding the constitutionality of the political editorializing and political attack rules suggests that the obligation to present opposing points of view must be applied to all constitutionally protected speech." Advertisements in the "editorial advertisement" category, defined as advertisements which consist of "direct and substantial commentary" on controversial issues of public importance, continue to be under the Fairness Doctrine.

**Advocacy.** At what point advocacy of the overthrow of government becomes punishable is not clearly defined in cases dealing with that question. One line of thought is that "...advocacy of violation, however reprehensible morally, is not a justification for denying free speech where the advocacy falls short of incitement and there is nothing to indicate that the advocacy would be immediately acted on. The wide difference between advocacy and incitement, between preparation and attempt, between assembling and conspiracy, must be borne in mind." *Whitney v. California*. Another point of view is: "Certainly an attempt to overthrow the Government by force, even though doomed from the outset because of inadequate numbers or power of the revolutionists, is a sufficient evil for Congress to prevent. The damage which such attempts create both physically and politically to a nation makes it impossible to measure the validity in terms of the probability of success, or the immediacy of a successful attempt." *Dennis v. United States*. As a generality, however, advocacy is protected by the First Amendment and incitement is not.

**A Fortiori.** A conclusion which logic dictates follows necessarily and with stronger force than another already accepted in the argument.

"Nor, a fortiori, does our decision authorize any restriction whatever, whether of content or layout, on stories or commentary originated by Pittsburgh Press, its columnists, or its contributors." *Pittsburgh Press v. Human Relations Commission.*

**Alleged.** To tag a defamatory accusation as "alleged" is not itself a defense against a libel action, but its inclusion may be relevant in particular cases. In a case involving an accusation of police misconduct, the U.S. Court of Appeals, Seventh Circuit, held that it was for the jury to determine whether Time's omission of "alleged" showed "actual malice." The U.S. Supreme Court disagreed: "Time's omission of the word 'alleged' amounted to the adoption of one of a number of possible rational interpretations of a document that bristled with ambiguities. The deliberate choice of such an interpretation, though arguably reflecting a misconception, was not enough to create a jury issue of 'malice' under New York Times." (The report so sharply criticized for ambiguous writing was a report of the United States Commission on Civil Rights.) The court went on to say: "We would add, however, a final cautionary note. Nothing in this opinion is to be understood as making the word 'alleged' a superfluity in published reports of information damaging to reputation. Our decision today is based on the specific facts of this case. . . ." *Time v. Pape.*

**Ambiguous Words.** In libel, if the words can be read two ways, one way defamatory, the other not, the jury determines which meaning was conveyed.

**Amicus Curiae.** A person or group who intervenes in a case with court permission to bring to the attention of the court some point of law or some germane interest which will be affected by the outcome of the case. For instance, in an antitrust action by the United States against the Associated Press, the American Newspaper Publishers Association was amicus curiae urging dismissal of the case and Field Enterprises, Inc. was amicus in support of the government. The phrase means "friend of the court." The plural is amici curiae.

**Ancillary Regulation.** Ancillary means "attendant upon." The U.S. Supreme Court in 1972 approved an FCC rule requiring nonbroadcast programming on some cable systems as within FCC authority because it was reasonably ancillary to the FCC's authority to assure that "in transmission of broadcast signals viewers are provided suitably diversified programming...." *United States v. Midwest Video*

*Corp.* Under this doctrine, the court decided that the Federal Radio Commission had power over intrastate radio as ancillary to authority over interstate radio, which devolves from the commerce clause of the federal constitution, because radio waves inside a state could affect radio waves crossing state lines. *Federal Radio Commission v. Nelson Brothers.*

**Anonymous Expression.** A Los Angeles ordinance banning handbills which did not identify a person as a source on the paper's cover or face was declared unconstitutional by the U.S. Supreme Court on the grounds that "such an identification would tend to restrict freedom to distribute information and thereby freedom of expression." Justice Hugo L. Black, for the 5-4 majority, praised the role of "anonymous pamphlets, leaflets, brochures and even books" in colonial America and in English history; and concluded "it is plain that anonymity has sometimes been assumed for the most constructive purposes." *Talley v. California.* Other justices did not find any "freedom of anonymity" in the constitution. Two years earlier, the court held that forced disclosure of membership lists of the National Association for the Advancement of Colored People was unconstitutional because economic and personal reprisals on individuals might follow. *NAACP v. Alabama.* Regardless of the majority's philosophy in *Talley*, source identification is required in political advertising of candidates for national office.

**Anonymous Work (Copyright).** A work on the copies or phonorecords of which no natural person is identified as the author.

**Antitrust.** Public policy expressed through federal statutes holds that competition in the marketplace of products and services is desirable and makes illegal business practices which improperly interfere with competition. The First Amendment grants no exemption from antitrust prosecutions for the business of publishing. "Freedom to publish is guaranteed by the Constitution, but freedom to combine to keep others from publishing is not. Freedom of the press from governmental interference under the First Amendment does not sanction repression of the interest by private interests." *Associated Press et al. v. United States.* See Newspaper Preservation Act. There also are state antitrust laws covering intra-state commerce.

**Appellant-Appelee.** The person who appeals from a lower to a higher court is the appellant; the appelee is the person against whom the appeal is taken. The appellant's name comes first in federal appeals because he's the one who lost in the next lower court. *New York Times v. Sullivan* before the U.S. Supreme Court reflects that the newspaper lost in the Alabama Supreme Court. State practices vary. Many states retain the original plaintiff's name as the first name regardless of who takes the appeal.

**Appellate Court.** A higher court with authority to change the decision of the lower court. An appellate court reviews the record of the trial court and determines whether error in substantive or adjective law requires a change of verdict. In the federal system, the district court is the court where the action begins (first jurisdiction). Appeals are taken to the U.S. Court of Appeals (which has jurisdiction over several districts) and from there to the U.S. Supreme Court. State court systems are similarly organized but the formal name of the court of original jurisdiction and of the appellate court or courts may vary. The higher the level of the court making the final decision, the more significant the decision becomes. U.S. Supreme Court decisions are the final word on the First Amendment.

**Appropriation.** A person has a property right to his or her own identity, and appropriation (use without permission) of a person's name or likeness is actionable as an invasion of privacy. This applies particularly to commercial use, but the concept is broader than that. "The fundamental wrong is the appropriation for one's self of the benefits of another's name, likeness, or identity, and the wrong is the same whether or not that benefit is pecuniary." *Zacchini v. Scripps-Howard.* Incidental use of name or likeness is not appropriation, nor is use for news purposes. The fact that newspapers and radio and television stations are profit-making enterprises does not translate their use of names in news contexts into a commercial use. See Right of Publicity.

**Areopagitica.** An essay by John Milton written in 1644 arguing for an end to the licensing of printers in England. Selected parts of it have been used since as a broad plea for freedom of expression, and particularly for tolerating error in debate on public issues. "And though all the winds of doctrine were let loose to play upon the earth, so truth be in the field, we do injuriously by licensing and prohibiting to misdoubt her strength. Let her and falsehood grapple; who ever knew truth put to the worse, in a free and open encounter." He excluded from his toleration "popery and open superstition" and writings "impious or evil . . . against faith or manners." The title comes from the court in ancient Greece, named Areopagiticus, revered for its integrity. The full formal title of the essay is: "Areopagitica; a Speech of Mr. John Milton For the Liberty of Unlicenc'd Printing, to the Parlament of England." He did not give it as a speech. His title indicates merely a literary form.

**Arguendo.** By way of argument. A judge sometimes uses the word to introduce an illustration of his reasoning by a hypothetical or parallel example.

**Attainder.** Extinction of the civil rights and the forfeiture of all real and personal property of a person judged guilty of treason or of a felony. A person so attained could not will property to another nor inherit property (called "corruption of blood") nor sue in court. A bill of attainder is a legislative act which bypasses any judicial action and imposes the penalties of attainder on a person directly. The Constitution specifically prohibits any bill of attainder.

**Attorney General.** The chief government attorney who advises the president, or the governor in an individual state, or legislators and departments of government in both areas, about legal matters affecting the government and represents these government officials and agencies in civil or criminal actions—usually at the appellate level. In the federal government, the attorney general is appointed by the president, and heads the department of justice. At state levels, he is in some places elected, in others appointed by the governor. Formal opinions by attorneys general usually have the force of law unless modified or rejected by a court.

**Audiovisual Works (Copyright).** Works that consist of a series of related images which are intrinsically intended to be shown by the use of machines or devices such as projectors, viewers, or electronic equipment, together with accompanying sounds, if any, regardless of the nature of the material objects, such as films or tapes, in which the works are embodied.

**Author.** In copyright, the word means more than a writer. The author is the creator of any copyrightable work. Thus, a sculptor is the author of the statue, the artist is the author of the painting.

**a**

**Average Person Test.** In *United States v. One Book Called Ulysses*, the judgment of obscenity was changed from the effect of such material on "the most susceptible person" to its effect on "a person with average sex instincts—what the French would call *l'homme moyen sensuel*—who plays in this branch of legal inquiry, the same role of hypothetical reagent as does the reasonable man in the law of torts . . . . " The decision also set the work as a whole, rather than an isolated passage, as a criterion for obscenity.

# b

**Bait and Switch.** A form of deceptive advertising in which a product at a bargain price (bait) induces the customer into the store where he finds the item conveniently "sold out" and a salesperson tries to persuade the customer to buy a higher-priced item (switch).

**Balancing Test.** Sometimes called the balance of interests doctrine, it describes one way of interpreting the First Amendment. Broadly, it means that a court balances freedom of expression against other societal rights, including private rights. Narrowly, it means that a court should take into careful account "the circumstances. . .and the substantiality of the reasons" for a legislative enactment infringing on expression. *Schneider v. United States.* Critics of the test, which at best is an imprecise guide, believe that it gives too much deference to the "balance" of competing interests already arrived at in the legislative process. And U.S. Supreme Court Justice Hugo L. Black believed that the authors of the First Amendment did all the balancing necessary when they wrote that no law should abridge freedom of expression. See Ad Hoc and Definitional Balancing.

**Best Edition (Copyright).** The edition, published in the United States at any time before the date of deposit of the work with the Office of Copyright, Library of Congress, which that office determines to be most suitable for recording the copyright.

**Bill of Rights.** The first 10 amendments to the Constitution. Adopted in 1791, these amendments set forth basic American freedoms, among them—freedom of speech, press, religion, and peaceful assembly to seek redress of grievances; freedom from compulsory testimony against oneself; freedom from unreasonable searches and seizures and the right to a trial by an impartial jury.

**Blackstone.** A respected English legal authority on the common law, the view of William Blackstone permeated much of the early thinking on freedom of expression. His theme is often quoted: "The liberty of the press is indeed essential to the nature of a free state; but this consists in laying no previous restraints upon publications, and not in freedom from censure for criminal matter when published." Anyone pub-

11

# b

lishing "what is improper, mischievous, or illegal" could be punished after the fact, but not restrained in advance of publication. Blackstone particularly found punishable "blasphemous, immoral, treasonable, schismatical, seditious, or scandalous libels." Although courts allow that prior restraint might be possible under extreme circumstances, the no restraint doctrine is fundamental to freedom of expression in the United States. More, the First Amendment is a broader grant of freedom than Blackstone's definition. The immunity from prior restraint "cannot be said to exhaust the conception of the liberty guaranteed by federal and state constitutions." *Near v. Minnesota.*

**Blue Book.** The popular name for Public Service Responsibility of Broadcast Licensees, a 1946 report of the Federal Communications Commission, which sets guidelines for programming in the public interest. The guidelines call for local live talent shows, programs on significant public issues and sustaining (non-sponsored) programs to achieve a balanced program diet. In 1960, the FCC issued another report on desirable programming standards, called the en Banc Programming Inquiry, which is relatively more enforced than the Blue Book was. It itemizes 14 types of programs which are "usually necessary" for the licensee to provide. These range from news, agriculture, weather and sports to religion, education, local talent and politics.

**Breach of the Peace.** Maintenance of "domestic tranquility" is a basic responsibility of government. Breaching the peace covers a litany of wrongs from disorderly conduct to a riot. Its application to media law is found in the reasoning underlying criminal libel—that words can provoke someone to breach the peace in retaliation. See Libel-Criminal.

**Breathing Space.** Freedom of expression needs some latitude of error permissible without punishment lest it be strangled by fear that the words or pictures printed or broadcast are too hazardous to risk. The "breathing space" description is sometimes used in First Amendment decisions as a reason for such latitude. See Self Censorship. "That erroneous statement is inevitable in free debate, and that it must be protected if the freedoms of expression are to have the 'breathing space' that they 'need . . . to survive' . . . ." *New York Times v. Sullivan.*

**Brief.** A lawyer's summary of facts and interpretations of law used to argue his case before an appellate court. Both sides prepare briefs, arguing from selections from relevant law cases those points which the lawyer believes will be persuasive for his side. Also, a summary of a law case, setting forth the issue, who won and who lost, and the reasoning of majority and minority views. Briefs are also used at the trial level, i.e. "Trial Brief."

**Burden of Proof.** If A accuses B of wrongdoing, the initial burden is on A to bring enough evidence to support a case. In libel, the burden goes first to the plaintiff to sustain that the words are defamatory, that he was identified and that the libel was published. The medium then has the burden of proving a defense—that the material is true, or falls within fair comment or is protected by qualified privilege. Public officials and public figures have an additional initial burden of proof—that the material was published with actual malice and therefore is not protected by the New York Times rule.

# C

**Cablecasting.** The origination of programming on a cable television system as distinct from the retransmission of signals that have been received over the air from conventional broadcast television stations. *Home Box Office v. FCC.*

**Cable TV System.** For its purposes, the FCC defines the term this way: A non-broadcast facility consisting of a set of transmission paths and associated signal generation, reception, and control equipment, under common ownership and control, that distributes or is designed to distribute to subscribers the signals of one or more television broadcast stations. Not included is any facility serving less than 50 subscribers or a facility serving only multiple unit dwellings under common control. The copyright law defines the term as: a facility, located in any state, territory, trust territory, or possession, that, in whole or in part, receives signals transmitted or programs broadcast by one or more television broadcast stations licensed by the FCC, and makes secondary transmission of such signals or programs by wires, cables, or other communications channels to subscribing members of the public who pay for such service.

**Calculated Falsehood.** One of several kinds of expression not protected by the First Amendment. "That speech is used as a tool for political ends does not automatically bring it under the protective mantle of the Constitution. For the use of the known lie as a tool is at once at odds with the premises of democratic government and with the orderly manner in which economic, social or political change is to be effected." *Garrison v. Louisiana.*

**Canon 20.** A 1908 American Bar Association ethical recommendation relating to comments by lawyers about trials. "Newspaper publications by a lawyer as to pending or anticipated litigation may interfere with a fair trial in the courts and otherwise prejudice the due administration of justice. Generally, they are to be condemned. If the extreme circumstances of a particular case justify a statement to the public, it is unprofessional to make it anonymously. An ex parte reference to the facts should not go beyond quotation from the records and papers on file in the court; but even in extreme cases it is better to avoid any ex parte statement." The ABA's Disciplinary Rule 7-107, adopted in many states, extends Canon 20 by restricting defense and prosecuting attorneys' comments essentially to the Katzenbach rules (which see).

**Canon 35.** This ethical recommendation adopted by the American Bar Association in 1937 recommends that cameras be barred from the courtroom because photography would "detract from the essential dignity of the proceedings, distract the participants and witnesses in giving testimony, and create misconceptions with respect thereto in the mind of the public." The canon exempts portions of naturalization proceedings. The revised version, 3(7), urges prohibition of "broadcasting, televising, recording, or taking photographs" but would permit television for internal court purposes (taking depositions, making a record of the trial) or closed-circuit television for educational use or to extend the visibility of the trial to other rooms in the courthouse for spectators or the press. A plurality of the U.S. Supreme Court justices in *Estes v. Texas* agreed with the reasoning underlying Canon 35 and would have made televising a trial a *per se* violation of a defendant's right to a fair trial. Media argue that modern equipment permits photos without distraction of participants or disruption of proceedings. Several states are permitting television of trials on an experimental basis but federal courts ban all still or television photography.

**CATV.** Community antenna television, or now, more commonly, cable television. In 1959, the Federal Communications Commission doubted it had authority to regulate cable, but as cable systems grew the FCC changed its mind and since 1966 has imposed various controls by finding that the communications act intended the FCC to adjust to developments not foreseeable when the act was passed in 1934. Such reasoning justifying authority over cable was upheld in *United States v. Southwestern Cable Co.* So, for examples, FCC rules govern cable use of distant signals which might adversely compete with a local broadcaster, limit concentration of ownership, and impose the Fairness Doctrine. In 1978, however, the U.S. Court of Appeals, Eighth Circuit, ruled that the agency went too far in a 1976 requirement that cable systems of more than 3,500 subscribers must provide four channels for public access. The court could find no ancillary connection to the FCC's accepted authority over broadcasting. The FCC had argued it was fulfiling the spirit of the First Amendment by enlarging opportunities for local expression. The court sharply reminded the agency that it was "the Federal Communications Commission, not the Federal First Amendment Commission." *Midwest Video v. FCC*. In cable, the FCC operates under a dualism policy which combines local franchising with FCC registration, compliance or licensing, depending on the size of the system. In 1976, of 3,450 systems nationally, 552 had more than 5,000 subscribers, but cable subscribers overall had risen from two to almost eleven million in the 1967-76 period.

**Case of First Impression.** When the issue before the court is novel and precedents are lacking, the judge sometimes will describe it as a "case of first impression.".

**Caveat Emptor.** "Let the buyer beware." Basically, it applies to advertising the laissez faire idea, i.e. let industry and business set their own rules without government interference and the market will sort the good from the bad. Caveat emptor was more than less the rule in the 18th and 19th centuries. Today it is not accepted under consumer protection laws nor Federal Trade Commission actions against deceptive advertising.

**Cease and Desist Order.** An order by a regulatory agency to a violator of a regulation to stop the violation. The Federal Trade Commission operates against deceptive advertising through cease and desist orders which are issued after a formal hearing and a finding that the advertisement is misleading. The order—a finding of "guilty" by the FTC—becomes effective after a 60-day grace period to allow for an appeal to a federal court, if the advertiser wants to. Violation of an effective cease and desist order is punishable by substantial fines for each day of subsequent use of the advertisement.

**Censorship.** An umbrella word covering different situations and ambiguous unless used in context. Censorship by government means variously a requirement that material be submitted to a government censor for approval before publication or the licensing of print media or taxation for the purpose of supressing freedom of expression. All such violate the First Amendment. The word includes prior restraint, i.e. injunctions restraining future publishing or broadcasting. Media also look on "gag orders" as censorship. Laws and decisions governing pornography are considered censorship by many critics, and some apply the word to non-governmental coercion of writers, publishers and broadcasters—the parents group that wants a book removed from a local school library, groups who pressure against the use of ethnic or racial terms which the group considers derogatory. At times, it is applied to laws restricting access to government records or to laws like the Official Secrets Acts in Britain which can punish media use of any material from a source unauthorized to release it. Censorship, at least in its narrow senses, contradicts this nation's commitment to a toleration of error in order that robust debate on public issues shall not be inhibited. The First Amendment, as U.S. Supreme Court Justice Hugo L. Black saw it, stands against almost all censorship because "it must be taken as a command of the broadest scope that explicit language, read in the context of a liberty-loving society, will allow." *Bridges v. California.*

**Certification Mark.** See Trademark.

**Certiorari.** To be informed or to be made certain of. It's the name of a writ from a higher to a lower court asking for the record of the case in order to review it. Certiorari granted by the U.S. Supreme Court means the court intends to rule on the matter. Cert. den. (denied) means that the highest previous verdict stands.

**Chain Broadcasting Regulations.** Rules of the Federal Communications Commission which cover items like network ownership of stations, terms of affiliation and territorial exclusivity, and which stand against network control of programming decisions by local licensees. These regulations were upheld in 1943 in *National Broadcasting Co. v. United States* as within the power of the FCC and as not violating any network's First Amendment rights to free speech. Chain broadcasting is defined in the Communications Act of 1934 as the "simultaneous broadcasting of an identical program by two or more connected stations."

**Chambers.** The private rooms in which a judge conducts the business of the court when he is not holding a formal session. Within chambers, a judge may hear motions, sign papers or discuss matters privately with attorneys or the plaintiff or defendant.

**Children (Copyright).** A person's immediate offspring, whether legitimate or not, and any children legally adopted.

**Chilling Effect.** Court interpretations which restrict the First Amendment or imprecise laws which leave ambiguous what is legal are sometimes said to have a "chilling effect" on freedom of expression. For example, a requirement that a publication or broadcast prove the literal truth of every assertion about a government official would have the "chilling effect" of restricting comment for fear of costly libel suits.

**Chrestensen Doctrine.** A holding, now outmoded, that advertising did not have First Amendment protection. It stems from a case turning on an attempt to gain First Amendment protection for a commercial handbill by adding a political protest to its other side. *Valentine v. Chrestensen.*

**Civil Action.** Legal action by one person against another seeking damages or some other redress of alleged injury. Criminal actions are brought in the name of the people against the individual, reflecting that crime is an injury to society at large. Civil actions are decided by preponderance of evidence. Criminal actions require proof beyond a reasonable doubt.

**Clear and Convincing Evidence.** To win a suit for libel, a public official or a public figure must prove actual malice by "clear and convincing evidence." As with other guide phrases, the words are imprecise but generally are taken to mean a standard of proof somewhere between the standard of a civil law suit (preponderance of evidence) and the standard in a criminal action (guilt beyond a reasonable doubt). Not all judges agree that the U.S. Supreme Court requires a "clear and convincing" standard. For example, Justice Quirico of the Massachusetts Supreme Judicial Court, in a dissent, wrote: "I do not agree that the United States Supreme Court has constitutionally mandated that the plaintiff prove malice in such a case by anything more than a fair preponderance of the evidence." He opined further that it's not possible to explain to a jury a standard as elusive as "clear and convincing." *Callahan v. Westinghouse Broadcasting.*

**Clear and Present Danger.** Set down originally in *Schenck v. United States,* this test says that words can be punished when they create a "clear and present danger that they will bring about the substantive evils that Congress has a right to prevent." Using that test, Schenck's conviction of conspiracy to violate the Espionage Act of 1917 was upheld. As with other formulas setting limits on the First Amendment, the phrase is elastic and depends on "circumstances," "proximity," and "degree." Subsequent interpretations have generally held it to require that "the substantive evil must be extremely serious and the degree of imminence extremely high before utterances can be punished." *Bridges v. California.* Critics like to point out that it can mean that precisely when words are effective and therefore dangerous they can be suppressed. As a test, clear and present danger has replaced the more restrictive rule of "reasonable tendency" in constructive contempt.

**Coins.** Motion picture films, slides, photographs and printed illustrations of United States and foreign coins may be used for any purpose, including advertising, according to a press guide booklet issued by the United States Secret Service, Department of the Treasury.

**Collective Mark.** See Trademark.

**Collective Work (Copyright).** A work, such as a periodical issue, anthropology, or encyclopedia, in which a number of contributions, constituting separate and independent works in themselves, are assembled into a collective whole.

**Commercial Speech.** The Chrestensen doctrine (1942) said that advertising was not protected by the First Amendment. In *New York Times v. Sullivan* (1964), the U.S. Supreme Court included under the First Amendment advertisements taking positions on public issues. In 1976, the court went further and ruled in a case involving prescription drug price advertising that "concededly truthful information about entirely lawful activity" could not be suppressed. *Virginia State Board of Pharmacy v. Virginia Citizens Consumer Council.* The court reasoned that commercial advertising is tied to self-government. ". . .the free flow of commercial information is indispensable . . . to the proper allocation of resources in a free enterprise system, it is also indispensable to the formation of intelligent opinions as to how the system ought to be regulated or altered. Therefore, even if the First Amendment were thought to be primarily an instrument to enlightened decision making in a democracy, we could not say that the free flow of information does not serve that goal." The court reasoned also that "speech does not lose its First Amendment protection because money is spent to project it." Further, "if there is a right to advertise, there is a reciprocal right to receive the advertising." Commercial speech therefore is now included in the First Amendment.

**Commission on Freedom of the Press.** Thirteen men appointed in 1944 by Robert Hutchins, then chancellor of the University of Chicago, to study the operative status of freedom of the press in the United States. The commission was financed by a $200,000 grant from Time, Inc.

# C

and $15,000 from the Encyclopedia Brittanica. The commission's report published in 1947, listed, among other things, its criteria of what the press should provide in a free society: 1. "A truthful comprehensive and intelligent account of the day's events in a context which gives them meaning." 2. "A forum for the exchange of comment and criticism." 3. "The projection of a representative picture the constituent groups in the society." 4. "The presentation and clarification of the goals and values of society." 5. "Full access to day's intelligence." The commission is sometimes called the Hutchins Commission.

**Commission on Obscenity.** Created by Congress in 1967, its members appointed by President Johnson, the commission concluded its work in 1970 with recommendations that all federal, state and local laws "prohibiting the sale, exhibition, or distribution of sexual materials to consenting adults" be repealed. Laws relating to children and obscenity were approved as were "unwarranted intrusions" of "explicit sexual materials" upon persons who didn't want such materials "thrust upon them." The commission's report had little or no effect on existing legislation. A stinging minority report attacked not only the legal conclusions but the technical validity of studies the commission undertook to gauge the effect of obscene materials on viewers. Its formal full title is The Commission on Obscenity and Pornography.

**Common Carrier.** Carriers are transportation and communications systems and are either private or common. If common, they accommodate indifferently those who seek their services. Broadcast licensees by specific statutory language are not common carriers; neither are newspapers. Were either considered common carriers, there would be an enforceable right of access to newspaper space and beyond the Fairness Doctrine to broadcasting time. See Public Utility.

**Common Law.** Law based on custom and usage in England and accumulated in the continuity of court decisions over time. American courts leaned heavily on English common law for precedents through the 19th century. The accumulation of court decisions in the United States has now established an American common law and English precedents are rarely used. Common law principles underlie many media law opinions, particularly in libel of private persons and in slander. The other main source of law is statutory law, i.e. law passed by a legislative body.

**Common Law Copyright.** The copyright which inheres in a manuscript from the moment of its creation until the work is published—at which

20

time it gains statutory copyright if published with a notice of copyright in the proper place. If published without copyright notice, the work goes into the public domain. Statutory copyright is the copyright granted under federal law. Common law copyright is eliminated in the 1978-effective revision of the copyright law whereby all future copyright is statutory.

**Communications Act of 1934.** The federal statute which created the Federal Communications Commission to replace the Federal Radio Commission and which centralized authority over radio (formerly first administered by the Secretary of Commerce and Labor and later by the FRC), over interstate common communication carriers (formerly under the Interstate Commerce Commission) and over certain cable and telegraph services, interstate and foreign.

**Community Ascertainment.** A Federal Communications Commission policy which requires an applicant for a license (new or renewal) to ascertain community needs by sampling a cross section of the general population and by interviews with diverse community leaders. The surveys are to determine community problems and to guide program decisions under the requirement that the licensee operate "in the public interest." Details on methodologies are spelled out in formal primers issued by the FCC.

**Compilation (Copyright).** A work formed by the collection and assembling of preexisting materials or of data that are selected, coordinated, or arranged in such a way that the resulting work as a whole constitutes an original work of authorship.

**Complaint.** In a civil action, a complaint is the first written pleading by a plaintiff in which he sets down his specific grievances against a defendant. In criminal law, it is the state filing a grievance against an individual for the people.

**Compulsory License (Copyright).** A provision whereby copyrighted material can be used without the author's permission provided a set fee is paid. Important in the new copyright law because therein it includes public TV's use of nondramatic literary, pictorial, musical or graphic works.

**Comstockery.** Anthony Comstock, a vigorous opponent of obscenity as then defined, successfully lobbied for a federal law against obscene writings or objects. The 1873 Comstock Law, amended several times,

# C

is the basic federal obscenity control act. Comstockery is usually used to connote an overzealous banning of lewd materials or to describe the actions of an overly censorial personality.

**Concurring Opinion.** An opinion agreeing with the majority opinion (the opinion of the court) but written either to emphasize different points or to agree with the majority's conclusion while disagreeing with the underlying reasoning.

**Consent Order.** One device used by the Federal Trade Commission to control advertising is an order whereby the advertiser agrees to cease a particular advertising message or practice but does not admit any legal violation by so doing. Stories about consent orders, therefore, should not be written as admissions of guilt. Consent decrees are also Court-sanctioned agreements in many areas wherein the parties accept the decree as justly determining their rights.

**Consent to Libel.** When a reporter gives a person accused of wrongdoing a chance to answer in the same story and the person does answer, the person is seen in some law decisions as having consented to the publication of the defamation. The Arkansas Supreme Court once expressed it this way in dismissing a libel case: "...we find it difficult to understand how one's denials to charges made can be published without also publishing the charges." *Brandon v. Gazette Publishing Co.* "No comment" is not considered consent. What does constitute consent is a subtle legal question and no reporter should depend on this doctrine without specific advice of an attorney.

**Constitutionally Vague.** Sometimes ordinances or statutes relating to First Amendment areas are unconstitutional because of "vagueness." This means that law is not sufficiently specific to enable a person of common intelligence to understand what is required or forbidden. A requirement that newsracks be maintained in "attractive condition" would be constitutionally vague because it involves "a totally subjective aesthetic judgment, "whereas the words "clean" and "neat" are held to be specific enough. Where "vagueness" begins and ends is itself vague and a matter for court judgment. *Kash Enterprises v. Los Angeles.*

**Contemner.** A person who has committed contempt of court.

**Contempt.** The power of a judge to punish someone who misbehaves in court, refuses to obey a court order, or degrades the court by accusatory words is considered an "inherent power" in the judiciary. The legitimacy of the roots of this "inherent power," allegedly found in English common law is disputed by scholars. See Wilmot's Doctrine. Whether or not well founded, it is now accepted as a power which courts must have to insure the integrity and dignity of the judicial process. The reasoning is that without such power orderly process and public acceptance of the court's role in the system of justice would be impossible. Contempt is modified in its application by federal and state statutes and by appellate decisions—covering such things as whether the contempt is tried before another judge, how far journalistic comment can go before being punishable, and the length of sentence that can be imposed without a trial by jury.

**Contempt—Civil, Criminal.** "Essentially, the difference between civil and criminal contempt is that the former seeks to change respondent's conduct by threatening him with a penalty if he does not change it, while the latter seeks to punish him for misdoings which affront the dignity of the court. Criminal contempt being for past misconduct, there is no way for one so convicted to purge himself of the contempt." *Jaikens v. Jaikens.* The difference is sometimes described by saying that the purpose of civil contempt is to remedy the wrong, of criminal contempt to punish the wrong. A person in civil contempt is said to hold the keys to the jail in that the contempt is removed when he agrees to obey the court.

**Contempt—Constructive, Direct.** Words spoken or written out of court which demean the court are constructive (or indirect) contempt and criminal contempt. Constructive contempt against a media person requires that the expression be a "clear and present danger" to the functioning of the court. That standard being difficult to meet, constructive contempt has fallen into disuse in the United States (but not in England where contempt against media is narrowly interpreted and vigorously applied). Direct contempt, usually civil contempt, is a front and center challenge to the court, for example, a reporter disobeying a gag order or refusing to testify when properly called to do so. The First Amendment does not exempt media from direct contempt; it does from constructive contempt up to the invisible line of the "clear and present danger" doctrine.

**Contempt—1831 Statute.** A federal law which limits the contempt power of the federal judiciary to "misbehavior in the courtroom or so near thereto" as to obstruct justice. One purpose of the statute was to limit constructive contempt actions by the federal bench. Similar laws for the same purpose were passed in a number of states. From 1919 to 1941, federal courts got around the statute through a U.S. Supreme Court decision that "so near thereto" meant cause-and-effect rather than geographical distance, which nicety of reasoning was rejected in the latter year and "so near thereto" was read to mean physical proximity. *Toledo Newspaper Co. v. United States* and *Nye v. United States*. A similar example of the judiciary not taking kindly to a legislature trying to limit constructive contempt (before the "clear and present danger" doctrine became controlling) is an Arkansas law which listed specific, direct contempts and said "no others" could be included. The Arkansas Supreme Court ruled, in effect, that under separation of powers it would decide what contempt included and not the legislature, and held a newspaper in contempt. *State v. Morrill*.

**Contempt—Summary.** The power of a judge to act directly and immediately to find a person guilty of contempt without normal procedural safeguards around the accused. It is now limited to extraordinary circumstances where immediate action to protect the court is not merely convenient but necessary. It applies where there is "such an open and serious threat to orderly procedure that instant and summary punishment, as distinguished from due and deliberate procedures" is required. *Harris v. United States*.

**Content Neutrality.** In order to avoid selective exclusion of unpopular ideas, government officials ought not to allow their attitude toward a subject or the style of expression to influence their decision whether to restrict it. "...regulation of communication may not be affected by sympathy or hostility for the point of view being expressed by the communicator." *Young v. American Mini Theatres, Inc.* Judges, of course, are human. Like objectivity for a journalist, content neutrality is desirable but not perfectly attainable.

**Continuance.** Postponement of a trial or other action pending before a court. The U.S. Supreme Court in *Sheppard v. Maxwell* named continuance as one of the powers the trial judge had (but did not use) to allow time for prejudice in the community against the defendant to die down. If continuances are prolonged, this suggested remedy would work against the defendant's right to a speedy trial.

**Contumely.** Insult, rudeness, humiliation. One of the words used in defining defamation.

**Copies (Copyright).** Material objects, other than phonorecords, in which a work is fixed by any method now known or later developed, and from which the work can be perceived reproduced, or otherwise communicated, either directly or with the aid of a machine or device. The term includes the material object, other than a phonorecord, in which the work is first fixed.

**Copyright.** A right granted by federal law (statutory copyright) to the owner of a copyrightable work to control its reproduction (subject to fair use or compulsory license exceptions). It's an intangible property right. Copyright stems from Article I, Section 8 of the Constitution which gives Congress the power ". . . to promote the progress of science and useful arts by securing for limited times to authors and inventors the exclusive right to their respective writings and discoveries." Its purpose is to spread knowledge by encouraging creativity. Prior to 1978, copyright endured for 28 years with an option of a 28-year renewal. The new copyright law sets the term at the life of the author plus 50 years. Previous copyrights which normally would have expired were extended by Congress so that works originally copyrighted in 1906 may still be under copyright. Works not in the public domain by Jan. 1, 1978, are extended on a formula which can add 75 years to the first copyright date. Copyright can be secured for a variety of creative works—from books to lectures to maps, music, drama, paintings, statues, photographs, motion pictures, sound recordings, designs, drawings and periodicals.

**Copyright Notice.** Three elements are required for a proper copyright notice. 1. The letter C inside a circle, or the word "Copyright" or the abbreviation "Copr." 2. The year of first publication (which may be omitted on pictorial, graphic or sculptural works reproduced on greeting cards, stationary, or in jewelry, dolls, toys, or any useful articles). 3. The name of the owner or an abbreviation of the name. Phonorecords require the letter P in a circle, the year of first publication and the name of the owner. No specific placement is required in literary copyright so long as it is located "as to give reasonable notice of the claim to copyright." However, the Register of Copyrights will recommend certain placements. The notice for phonorecords must be placed "on the surface of the phonorecord, or on the phonorecord label or container" in a position to give "reasonable notice" that the work is copyrighted.

**Copyright Royalty Tribunal.** A tribunal of five persons appointed by the president with senate approval for a term of seven years each. It determines royalty rates for the use of certain copyrighted materials which come under compulsory licensing (e.g. public performances of non-

# C

dramatic musical works on coin-operated players) and certain uses by cable television systems. The tribunal is authorized by the new copyright law effective Jan. 1, 1978.

**Corporations—First Amendment.** The Massachusetts Supreme Judicial Court ruled in 1977 that a corporation's First Amendment rights are limited to influencing issues which directly affect its business, property or assets. The court upheld a Massachusetts statute which prohibited corporations from spending money to influence votes on issues other than those "materially affecting" the corporation. The U.S. Supreme Court disagreed. In a case of first impression, Justice Lewis F. Powell, Jr., in the opinion of the court, could ". . . find no support in the First or Fourteenth Amendments . . . for the proposition that speech that otherwise would be within the protection of the First Amendment loses that protection simply because its source is a corporation that cannot prove, to the satisfaction of a court, a material effect on its business or property." And, "the inherent worth of the speech in terms of its capacity for informing the public does not depend upon the identity of its source, whether corporation, association, union, or individual." And, "If the speakers here were not corporations, no one would suggest that the state could silence their proposed speech. It is the type of speech indispensable to decision making in a democracy, and this is no less true because the speech comes from a corporation rather than an individual." The decision carefully refrained from deciding whether corporations ". . .have the full measure of rights that individuals enjoy under the First Amendment." But the decision did give First Amendment protection to corporations seeking to influence public opinion on general ballot issues. *First National Bank of Boston v. Bellotti.*

**Corporation for Public Broadcasting.** An agency set up by Congress in 1969 to supply, through the Public Broadcasting Service, programming for non-commercial, educational radio and television stations. It is funded largely by the federal government. Supplementary funding comes from foundations or citizen contributions. A board of 15-persons, appointed by the president with the advice and consent of the senate for six-year terms, governs its policies.

**Corrective Advertising.** A policy begun by the Federal Trade Commission in 1971 under which an advertiser can be required for a period of time to correct in subsequent ads misleading parts of ads previously published or broadcast. An illustrative example is found in *Warner-Lambert v. Federal Trade Commission.* The FTC had ordered the company to cease and desist from representing that Listerine will cure

26

or prevent colds or sore throats. The same order required that "the next ten million dollars of Listerine advertising" include these words: "Contrary to prior advertising, Listerine will not help prevent colds or sore throats or lessen their severity." The U.S. Court of Appeals, District of Columbia, ruled that the first four words—contrary to prior advertising—went too far, but approved the rest of the wording of the corrective order. The court found the FTC standard for judging when corrective advertising could apply to be "entirely reasonable." "If a deceptive advertisement has played a substantial role in creating or reinforcing in the public's mind a false and material belief which lives on after the false advertising ceases, there is clear and continuing injury to competition and to the consuming public as consumers continue to make purchasing decisions based on the false belief. Since the injury cannot be averted by merely requiring respondent to cease disseminating the advertisement, we may appropriately order... affirmative action designed to terminate the otherwise continuing ill effects of the advertisement." The court rejected Warner-Lambert's claim that because "the Supreme Court has recently extended First Amendment protection to commercial advertising, mandatory corrective advertising is unconstitutional." The court pointed out that the Supreme Court in *Virginia State Board v. Virginia Citizens Consumer Council* had "expressly noted that the First Amendment presents 'no obstacle' to government regulation of false or misleading advertising."

**Counter Advertising.** A term describing a 1972 Federal Trade Commission recommendation to the Federal Communications Commission that the FCC require broadcasters to sell or give time for direct rebuttal to advertisements impinging on controversial public issues, e.g. auto safety, nutrition, pollution. The proposal has not been implemented. The FCC does, however, apply the Fairness Doctrine to editorial advertising, i.e. advertising designed primarily as commenting on a public issue. In 1966, counter advertising was imposed by court order but held to cigarette advertising only on the grounds that since federal policy declared cigarettes to be a health hazard, anti-cigarette views had a right to be heard under the Fairness Doctrine. *Banzhaf v. FCC.* Subsequently (1971), Congress prohibited any advertising of cigarettes over licensed media. The concept of counter advertising is on shaky grounds under the reasoning in *Columbia Broadcasting System v. Democratic National Committee* wherein the U.S. Supreme Court ruled against any right of access on demand for advertising in licensed media. The court opined that such a right would

# C

infringe upon the First Amendment right of a licensee to make decisions on his station's programming within the boundaries of the Fairness Doctrine.

**Created (Copyright).** A work is created when it is fixed in a copy or a
phonorecord for the first time. Where a work has been prepared over
a period of time, the portion of it that has been fixed at any particular
time constitutes the work as of that time. Where the work has been
prepared in different versions, each version constitutes a separate
version.

**Cross Ownership.** Common ownership of a newspaper and a broadcasting station in the same community of license. In 1975, the Federal
Communications Commission banned any future cross-ownerships,
ordered 16 to be broken up, and allowed others to continue unless it's
clearly shown that "cross ownership harms the public interest." The
U.S. Court of Appeals, District of Columbia, upheld the ban on any
future cross ownerships but turned around the FCC policy regarding
existing combinations. The court ordered divestiture unless the "evidence clearly discloses that cross-ownership is in the public interest."
The court saw mandatory divestiture as good public policy because
"it increases the possibility that the public will be served by broadcasters with diverse views." *National Citizens Committee for Broadcasters v. FCC.* The U.S. Supreme Court accepted the FCC's 1975
order rather than the position of the Court of Appeals.

**Custom and Usage.** Certain actions acquire at least a premise of legal
validity if they have a tradition behind them and no protests have been
made against such actions. By common practice and acceptance they
acquire legitimacy. Thus, the Florida Supreme Court held that a
newspaper photographer was not liable for trespass for entry into and
picture taking in a fire-damaged home when the photographer entered
with police and fire officers under circumstances that were "common
custom and usage" in news reporting. *Florida Publishing Co. v.
Fletcher.*

28

# d

**Damages.** Money awarded by a court to compensate for an injury to a person, his property, or rights. In First Amendment law cases, damages are awarded in successful libel, invasion of privacy, or infringement of copyright suits.

**Deceptive Advertising.** The Federal Trade Commission uses a number of standards to judge when an advertisement is deceptive. Among them: the effect of the overall impression of the advertisement on an inexpert reader; interpretation of ambiguous words or phrases, one meaning true, the other false, in their false meaning; the advertisement's capacity to deceive with neither intention to deceive nor actual deception needing to be shown; whether a statement even though true adequately supports the overall claim, and whether omission of information creates a deceptive impression. Words are interpreted in their common meaning.

**Decision.** A word which media frequently use interchangeably with judgment or opinion. More exactly, the decision or disposition is the conclusionary action of a competent tribunal (the verdict); judgment or holding is more closely tied to those summary legal words preceding "affirmed" or "reversed" (or other disposition); and opinion is more the overall body of reasoning. Thus, *Sheppard v. Maxwell* begins with "Mr. Justice Clark delivered the opinion of the court," which opinion finds the press guilty of excesses in prejudical publicity and the judge lax in using the powers he had to protect Sheppard's right to a fair trial. The judgment, then, appears at the end: "Since the state trial judge did not fulfill his duty to protect Sheppard from the inherently prejudicial publicity which saturated the community...." The decision then follows that Sheppard be either released or retried. Trial courts act through orders or judgments. An appeal is from the final order or judgment of the trial court, which explains its reasoning in an opinion. Appeal courts enter opinions which conclude in judgments affirming or reversing, and enter orders based on the decision. The words— order, judgment, opinion—are capitalized in formal legal usage.

**Declaratory Judgment.** A court decision defining the rights of parties in a dispute or expressing an opinion on a question of law, which decision requires no performance by the parties nor orders relief such as an injunction or damages.

**Defamation.** Exposing another "to public hatred, shame, obloguy, contumely, odium, contempt, ridicule, aversion, ostracism, degradation, or disgrace, or to induce an evil opinion of one in the mind of right-thinking persons and to deprive one of their confidence and friendly intercourse in society." *Kimmerle v. New York Evening Journal.* Defamation is the broad term. Libel and slander are forms of defamation.

**Defendant.** The person against whom a civil or criminal action is brought. The bringer of the action is the plaintiff. Media usage generally holds plaintiff to civil suits and uses "the prosecution" or "prosecutor" in criminal actions. In a criminal case, law terms the defendant a "respondent" but media use defendant.

**Definitional Balancing.** A way of interpreting the First Amendment wherein the balancing is not to determine whether other rights should prevail in a particular case but to determine initially whether the expression itself is within First Amendment protection. Thus, obscenity is defined as expression not within the First Amendment on a "balancing" that only expression with some social value is protected. The other "balancing" approach is seen, for example, in cases where a court weighs a citizen's responsibility to testify when properly called on against a claimed right to a confidence privilege and the relevance and need for that testimony in that particular case. The definitional approach has the virtue of clarifying what's in and out of protected expression, and the defect that future decisions might define more out than in.

**De Minimis.** A Latin term used by courts to say that the law does not deal with trifles or irrelevant material.

**De Novo.** Latin for afresh or anew. Courts use it when ordering a new trial as in "trial de novo," meaning the case starts all over again.

**Derivative Work (Copyright).** A work based upon one or more preexisting works, such as a translation, musical arrangement, dramatization, fictionalization, motion picture version, sound recording, art reproduction, abridgment, condensation, or any other form in which a work may be recast, transformed or adapted. A work consisting of editorial revisions, annotations, elaborations, or other modifications which, as a whole, represent an original work of authorship, is a derivative work.

**Detroit Ordinance.** An ordinance, first passed in Detroit, which controls the number and location of sex-oriented businesses by zoning. Upheld by the U.S. Supreme Court in *Young v. American Mini Theatres* as not infringing the First Amendment, the ordinance requires that such places be separated by 1,000 feet and that a new enterprise obtain approval of 51 percent of the residents within a 500-foot radius if it is to locate in a residentially-zoned area. Places in existence before the ordinance was passed in 1972 are exempt. The 1,000-foot restriction breaks up "sin strips" when an "adult" store or movie goes out of business, and the 51 percent requirement tends to prevent the neighborhood blight which such enterprises are accused of encouraging.

**Deviant Group Test.** A standard for judging obscenity. "Where the material is designed primarily for and primarily disseminated to a clearly defined deviant sexual group, rather than to the public at large, the prurient-appeal requirement of the Roth test is satisfied if the dominant theme of the material taken as a whole appeals to the prurient interest of the members of that group." *Mishkin v. New York.*

**Directed Verdict.** Under some circumstances and based on his knowledge of law, a judge can order a jury to decide a case in a certain way. In effect, he takes the decision out of the jury's hands and makes it for them.

**Dismissal With Prejudice.** This phase attached to the resolution of a law case bars any further action on the same claim or cause. Dismissal without prejudice does not. For example, a case involving an effort by the St. Louis Globe-Democrat to gain access to certain police records was dismissed by the federal district court without prejudice because Missouri courts were adjudicating the same questions which involved, in part, the Missouri state constitution.

**Disparagement.** False statements adverse to products or property made to third parties with intent to cause monetary damage. The plaintiff must prove actual damages, falsity and malice. Disparagement can spill over into defamation. The two are closely allied and hard to distinguish.

# d

**Display (Copyright).** To show a copy of a work, either directly or by means of a film, slide, television image, or any other device or process or, in the case of a motion picture or other audiovisual work, to show individual images nonsequentially.

**Dissent.** The statement by a judge or justice disagreeing with a majority decision. Since the personnel of the U.S. Supreme Court changes over time, or an individual justice changes his mind, well reasoned dissents sometimes emerge as the basis for later majority decisions. Several may join in a dissent—thus, Mr. Justice Stewart, whom Mr. Justice Black, Mr. Justice Brennan and Mr. Justice White join, dissenting, means Justice Stewart is writing the dissent and the others are agreeing with him; or there can be as many separately written dissents as dissenters. The other side of the coin is—Mr. Chief Justice Warren, whom Mr. Justice Douglas and Mr. Justice Goldberg join, concurring, which means those three justices agree with "the opinion of the court" written by Mr. Justice Clark, but either disagree with Justice Clark's reasons for the same conclusion or wish to emphasize different points or to add new ones. (Example from *Estes v. Texas).*

**Distribution.** The First Amendment covers more than just freedom to speak and to write. "Liberty of circulation is as essential to that freedom as liberty of publishing; indeed, without the circulation, the publication would be of little value." *Ex Parte Jackson.* Distribution, however, can be subject to regulations concerning time, place and manner.

**Diversity Action.** Legal actions brought in federal court between parties who are residents of different states. The Judiciary Act of 1789 grants federal court jurisdiction in such cases. The underlying theory was that one state might be prejudiced against citizens of another state, given the greater sense of states' rights then prevailing, and that a federal court in such disputes would be more neutral. Chief Justice Warren E. Burger favors eliminating diversity actions as a reform to ease the federal docket of cases (in 1977, one in five of federal court cases arose from diversity actions). Congress has considered several such proposals, one compromise suggested being that the defendant but not the plaintiff could take the diversity route. Elimination of diversity is opposed by those who see the federal court as an escape from unevenness in quality of courts among the states.

**Duopoly Rule.** A Federal Communications Commission rule that it will not permit a licensee to acquire a second radio broadcasting license where the second service area would overlap the first. AM-FM radio combinations are not barred but are to be carefully reviewed. In 1970, the FCC moved to a one-to-a-customer rule, denying thereafter an AM radio license to a VHF (TV) license holder and vice versa, but requiring no divestiture of such combinations then existing and promising careful examination of any future applications involving radio and UHF (TV) combinations. Cross ownership of broadcasting and newspaper outlets in the same area were banned in 1975 but almost all such existing combinations were grandfathered in.

# e

**Editorializing by Licensees.** Arguing that "the broadcaster cannot be an advocate," the Federal Communications Commission in 1941 banned editorializing. In 1949, it agreed to editorializing subject to the Fairness Doctrine. In 1960, the FCC included editorializing as an affirmative element to be used, among others, in judging whether the station was operating in the public interest. Editorializing is therefore more than permitted, it is encouraged.

**Election Day Editorials.** To ban editorials about candidates or issues printed on election day on the grounds that such a ban is a reasonable restriction which prevents last-minute unanswerable attacks is unconstitutional. Alabama had such a law. "The Alabama Corrupt Practices Act by providing criminal penalties for publishing editorials (on election day) silences the press at a time when it is most effective. It is difficult to conceive of a more obvious and flagrant abridgment of the constitutionally guaranteed freedom of the press." *Mills v. Alabama*.

**En Banc Programming.** See Blue Book.

**Et Al.** Abbreviation of et (and) alius (another) or alii (others). When multiple names are plaintiffs or defendants in a law case, et al. is used after the first named person to obviate repetitive listing of all the names.

**Equal Time.** The Communications Act (Section 315) requires a licensee who permits a "legally qualified candidate" to appear on radio or television to make equal opportunities available to other candidates for the same office (in a primary, only other candidates of the same party). Free time must be matched with free time and paid time matched by the opportunity to buy paid time at the same rate. The time allotted must allow for a comparable audience. A Sunday morning slot is not equal to prime hours. Only candidates, not spokespersons for candidates, are eligible for equal time. Exempted from the requirement by a 1959 amendment to the act are bona fide newscasts, news interviews, news documentaries and breaking news events. The licensee is prohibited any "power of censorship over the material broadcast" under the equal time provision.

# e

**Executive Order 11652.** An order by President Nixon concerning classification and declassification of national security information. The order permits classification of documents as confidential, secret or top secret in the interests of national defense or foreign relations and provides for orderly declassification. Executive orders of this nature began in 1951 with President Truman who applied the Army and Navy classifications from World War II to document classifications in the executive branch, and a similar order was issued by President Eisenhower. National security, a phrase broader than national defense or foreign relations has become the operative word by which the executive justifies classification.

**Executive Privilege.** The alleged right of the president under separation of powers to withhold documents from examination and executive personnel from questioning by Congress. Several presidents have asserted the privilege, President Eisenhower among them, when he refused information sought by Senator Joseph McCarthy. President Nixon, in a statement of March 12, 1973, said "the doctrine is rooted in the Constitution which vests 'the executive power' solely in the president, and is designed to protect communications within the executive branch in a variety of situations in time of both war and peace." Several constitutional scholars dispute the historical or constitutional legitimacy of the doctrine. Applied to withholding information from the judiciary, the doctrine was tested in *Nixon v. United States*. The U.S. Supreme Court said: "However, neither the doctrine of separation of powers, nor the need for confidentiality of high-level communications, without more, can sustain an absolutely unqualified presidential privilege of immunity from judicial process under all circumstances." The court noted that the case before it did not present "a claim of need to protect military, diplomatic or sensitive national security secrets" and so did not rule whether executive privilege might apply thereto. Events surrounding President Nixon's departure from office have made the doctrine politically controversial and it likely will continue so for some years to come. In another context, the term relates to immunity for libel by members of the executive branch of government.

**Exclusivity Protection.** A television station in the top 50 markets can hold an exclusive right to show a particular program or series for the term of its contract with the provider of the program, and in the second 50 markets can hold exclusivity for two years. Exclusivity bars a cable system from importing the program from another market into the protected market. Exclusivity arrangements are used also in syndicated print materials, giving one newspaper exclusive rights to a particular columnist within its circulation area, for example. The degree to which this can be done is a question under antitrust laws.

**Exhaustion Doctrine.** News handlers (or anyone else) should in the eyes of the law go through an appeals process, that is, exhaust whatever remedies there may be in law itself, before they decide whether to disobey a court order. The point is illustrated in *United States v. Dickinson*. Two reporters who defied a federal district court order which was declared unconstitutional on appeal were held in contempt for defying the original order because they had not exhausted their remedies within the judiciary. The doctrine applies also to remedies within administrative agencies.

**Ex Parte.** A legal action on the application of one party only, for example, a temporary restraining order on behalf of X to stop Y from some action. Ex parte orders are granted in limited situations to prevent irreparable harm. Because the other party is not present at the time of entry of the order, a hearing is required to be held within a short time after the ex parte order is issued.

**Ex Rel.** Legal action brought by an attorney general on behalf of the state but on information provided by another person properly interested in the matter. The full title of the landmark prior restraint case is *Near v. Minnesota ex rel. Olson*. Olson was Floyd B. Olson, a county prosecutor. Rel. abbreviates relatione (related to).

**Extreme Departure Test.** In *Curtis Publishing Co. v. Butts,* a libel case, a plurality of justices, but not a majority, opted for a new rule under which a public figure who was not a public official could win damages in a libel suit. The test would be whether evidence would support "a showing of highly unreasonable conduct constituting an extreme departure from the standards of investigation and reporting ordinarily adhered to by responsible publishers." This approach to distinguishing public figures from public officials has not been supported in subsequent decisions. The U.S. Supreme Court endorsed in the later *Gertz v. Welch* case the actual malice standard of *New York Times v. Sullivan* as applying also to public figures.

# f

**Fair Comment.** Writers and broadcasters have a right to comment on the performance of anyone offering himself or herself for public approval. Theatrical and sports personalities, authors and artists, public officials, community leaders affecting issues of public concern—all can be criticized without jeopardy provided the opinion given is based on the facts of the public offering and is made without malice. Fair comment is a defense against libel suits based on such opinions. Truth is the defense against a libel suit based on the underlying fact (modified for public officials and public figures by the New York Times rule). The word fair need not mean calm and judicious. It also covers caustic criticism, sarcasm, severe condemnation, aggressive attack. Alleging corrupt motives against the public performer can undermine the defense in that it may move the issue from an opinion to a fact.

**Fair Use.** Some uses of copyrighted material do not constitute infringement. This exemption covers limited use for criticism, comment, news reporting, teaching, scholarship, or research. Four standards are used to judge whether the usage is fair use in any particular instance: the nature of the copyrighted work; how much is used; the effect on the market for the work; and the purpose and circumstances surrounding the use, particularly whether the use is for commercial or nonprofit educational purposes. Fair use conditions for reproduction by libraries and archives, for certain performances and displays and for secondary transmissions are set forth at length in the 1978 copyright law. Previous copyright laws did not mention fair use, but the doctrine was inserted by court decisions under the reasoning that the spread of knowledge "would be frustrated if the useful knowledge could not be used without incurring the guilt of piracy . . . ." *Baker v. Selden.*

**Fairness Doctrine.** In 1959, Congress exempted news programs from the equal time requirement and added to Section 315 of the Communications Act of 1934 language which succinctly expresses the Fairness Doctrine. The new language emphasizes that licensees have "the obligation imposed upon them under this act to operate in the public interest and to afford reasonable opportunity for the discussion of conflicting views on issues of public importance." Fairness imposes

# f

an affirmative duty on licensees to present balanced coverage of issues. It does not require explicit balancing of views within an individual program, but over time the licensee should give different views a chance to be heard. The licensee determines which are "issues of public importance" and the amount of programming time to be devoted to them. One expression of the doctrine can be found in a 1929 statement of the Federal Radio Commission: "Insofar as a program consists of discussion of public questions, the public interest requires ample play for the free and fair competition of opposing views. . . ." In 1949, the FCC stated the doctrine in words similar to the 1959 amendment. Critics argue that the doctrine tends to inhibit controversial programming because the licensee has less problems in balancing if such programs are kept to a minimum. The doctrine is further attacked as infringing on First Amendment rights of licensees to make editorial judgments. Its constitutionality, however, has been upheld under the reasoning: "It is the right of the viewers and listeners, not the right of the broadcasters, which is paramount." *Red Lion Broadcasting v. FCC.* More specific extensions of the concept are equal time and personal attack.

**False Light.** A term which applies to an invasion of privacy by way of fictionalization or other rearrangements of underlying facts or by way of out-of-context use of a person's name or picture. In *Time v. Hill,* the underlying facts of a family held hostage by escaping convicts were reshaped for use in a dramatic play but the court ruled that such fictionalization did not reach the reckless-disregard standard used to determine liability when public figures are involved. Reuse of a news picture in a different context could put the subject into a "false light" by creating a different impression than the original picture justified.

**Family Viewing Policy.** A policy adopted in 1975 by broadcasting networks through pressure from the Federal Communications Commission which banned programs inappropriate for general family viewing from the first hour of prime time and the hour immediately preceding. If broadcast, the viewers were to be alerted before the program began. The policy was ruled unconstitutional as a violation of the First Amendment because the networks failed to resist the FCC coercion and also infringed upon the First Amendment right of the individual station licensee to make program decisions. *Writers Guild v. FCC.*

**Famosus Libellus.** Written defamation or libel as distinct from injuria verbalis, oral defamation or slander.

**f**

**Federal Communications Commission.** Established by the Communications Act of 1934, this seven-person agency issues licenses, allocates frequencies, and regulates the use of public air waves. Its members are appointed by the president with advice and consent of the Senate for terms of seven years. The FCC has quasi-judicial and legislative powers and operates through rules and regulations formally issued after hearings. FCC administrative law judges, independent of the commission, rule on disputes about regulations and can issue interlocutory orders (temporary orders on some points pending decision on the whole issue). Appeals from FCC decisions are heard by a U.S. Court of Appeals. FCC's licensing and regulatory powers are not a denial of First Amendment rights, but the commission is barred from choosing "among applicants upon the basis of their political, economic or social views, or upon any other capricious basis." *National Broadcasting Co. v. United States.*

**Federal Election Campaign Act.** A 1971 law which requires broadcasters to allow legally qualified candidates for any federal elective office "reasonable access" to free or purchased time. The intent of the law is to prevent a broadcaster from getting around the equal time requirement by denying any candidate entry to his broadcasting facility.

**Federal Radio Commission.** Set up by the Radio Act of 1927, this commission evolved into the Federal Communications Commission. Its powers of licensing and to license and regulate were basically the same as the present FCC. It had five members appointed by the president with the advice and consent of the senate.

**Federal Trade Commission.** Created by Congress in 1914 to augment antitrust policy by controlling unfair methods of competition in commerce, this agency attempts to eliminate deceptive advertising. By the Wheeler-Lea Act of 1938, its powers were increased by adding to "unfair methods of competition in commerce" the words "and unfair or deceptive acts or practices in commerce." ". . . the commission could thenceforth prevent unfair or deceptive acts or practices in commerce which injuriously affect the public interest alone, while under the original act the commission's power to safeguard the public against unfair trade practices depended upon whether the objectionable acts or practices affected competition." *Scientific Manufacturing co. v. FTC.* This substantial change enabled the FTC to move against deceptive advertising as a protection of consumers regardless of the advertisement's effect on competition. The president with ad-

vice and consent of the senate appoints its five members for seven
year terms.

**Fiduciary.** A relationship wherein one person acts as a trustee for another and accords the other fidelity and loyalty. Chief Justice Warren
Burger for the court in *Miami Herald v. Tornillo* mentioned this relationship as one of the arguments advanced for an enforceable right of
access to print media, which the court unanimously turned down. "It
is urged that the claim of newspapers to be 'surrogates for the public'
carries with it a concomitant fiduciary obligation to account for that
stewardship. From this premise it is reasoned that the only effective
way to insure fairness and accuracy and to provide for some account-
ability is for government to take affirmative action." Two years later
in *Nebraska Press Association v. Stuart*, Justice Burger used the
same term in a more affirmative tone of voice. "The extraordinary
protections afforded by the First Amendment carry with them something in the nature of a fiduciary duty to exercise the protected rights
responsibly—a duty widely acknowledged but not always observed
by editors and publishers." The fiduciary obligation is used as one
supporting reason for judicial approval of the Fairness Doctrine in
licensed media. Justice Byron White wrote in *Red Lion Broadcasting
v. FCC:* "There is nothing in the First Amendment which prevents
the government from requiring a licensee to share his frequency with
others and to conduct himself as a proxy or fiduciary with obligations
to present those voices and views which are representative of his
community . . . ." In short, a fiduciary relationship, which connotes
enforceable duties, between media and their audience has been applied to broadcast but not to print media.

**Fighting Words.** A statute in New Hampshire which made punishable
any words so provocative as to invite a violent response was held
constitutional by the U.S. Supreme Court in 1942. The test, the court
said, is what "men of common intelligence would understand to be
words likely to cause an average addressee to fight." The court reasoned that "such utterances are no essential part of any exposition of
ideas" and are of "slight social value as a step to truth." *Chaplinsky
v. New Hampshire.* Seven years later, holding a Chicago ordinance
invalid, the court distinguished direct fighting words from speech
which invites dispute by the sensitivity of the issue and the quality of
the speaker's language. "...a function of free speech under our system
of government is to invite dispute. It may indeed best serve its high
purpose when it induces a condition of unrest, creates dissatisfaction
with conditions as they are, or even stirs people to anger." *Terminiello v. Chicago.* But in *Feiner v. New York*, the high court made

clear that the speaker could be arrested when he is inciting a riot. "It is one thing to say that the police cannot be used as an instrument for the suppression of unpopular views, and another to say that, when as here the speaker passes the bounds of argument or persuasion and undertakes incitement to riot, they are powerless to prevent a breach of the peace." The question of provocative speech is a sensitive one because it arises usually around controversial speakers in times of public tensions over an issue.

**Filming Executions.** Under the reasoning that "the First Amendment does not guarantee the press a constitutional right of special access to information not available to the public generally," the U.S. Court of Appeals, Eighth Circuit, overruled the U.S. District Court for the Northern District of Texas which had ordered Texas to allow filming of an execution. Texas allows reporters access to executions but bans filming or recording of the spectacle. *Garrett v. Estelle.*

**First Amendment.** "Congress shall make no law respecting an establishment of religion, or prohibiting the free exercise thereof; or abridging the freedom of speech, or of the press; or the right of the people peaceably to assemble, and to petition the government for a redress of grievances." Media's concern lies primarily in the speech-press part of the amendment, which is now interpreted to cover motion pictures, radio and television and advertising, but each form of expression is not covered in exactly the same way. The word "press" includes also handbills, pamphlets etc. James Madison is the principal author of the amendment. Scholars dispute what extensions of its meaning were in the minds of the congressmen who recommended it to the states or of the states which ratified it. Almost all significant First Amendment decisions by the U.S. Supreme Court have been made in the last half-century or so, particularly since 1925 when the court ruled the First Amendment binding on state governments as well as the federal government. The court has consistently held that the First Amendment is "not an absolute" but is limited by other societal needs.

**Fixed (Copyright).** A work is fixed in a tangible medium of expression when its emodiment in a copy or a phonorecord, by or under the authority of the author, is sufficiently permanent or stable, to permit it to be perceived, reproduced or otherwise communicated for a period of more than transitory duration. A work consisting of sounds, images, or both, that are being transmitted, is "fixed" if a fixation of the work is being made simultaneously with its transmission.

# f

**Fixed Mileage Zones.** Areas in which microwave served cable systems of more than 1,000 subscribers have limitations imposed by the Federal Communications Commission on importing distant signal network programs. The zones are a 35-mile radius (3,850 square miles) of protection for regular stations in the 100 largest markets and a 55-mile radius (9,500 square miles) for all others. The purpose of the zones is to protect the market for a network affiliate's network programming. The fixed mileage zones, adopted in 1975, replaced a previous system of zones based on "contour strength," essentially signal strength. The FCC can adjust zones as circumstances warrant.

**FM Broadcast Band.** "Consists of that portion of the radio frequency spectrum between 78 megacycles per second and 108 MC/s. It is divided into 100 channels of 200 kilocycles per second each." *Title 47 C.F.R. 73.201.*

**Fourteenth Amendment.** Added to the federal constitution in 1868, this amendment is the vehicle by which the First Amendment now applies to state governments. (When adopted in 1791, the First Amendment applied only to the federal government.) The fourteenth says in part: "No state shall make or enforce any law which shall abridge the privileges or immunities of citizens of the United States; nor shall any state deprive any person of life, liberty, or property, without due process of law; nor deny to any person within its jurisdiction the equal protection of the laws." In *Gitlow v. New York,* the U.S. Supreme Court applied the fourteenth in this statement: "For present purposes we may and do assume that freedom of speech and of the press—which are protected by the First Amendment from abridgement by Congress—are among the fundamental personal rights and 'liberties' protected by the due process clause of the Fourteenth Amendment from impairment by the states."

**Fox Libel Act.** Passed by the British Parliament in 1792, the act made truth a defense in sedition—contrary to the earlier doctrine "the greater the truth, the greater the libel." The act also gave the jury the right to judge whether the material was in fact defamatory rather than merely deciding whether the defendant had published it, the latter being the rule that British courts had tried to impose through common law on earlier juries. Today, the doctrine that the truth could be seditious is unaccepted and juries commonly judge the degree of defamation under rules of law set down by the judge.

**Freedom of Information Act.** Passed by Congress in 1966, this law opens federal government records to public inspection with nine exceptions involving national security, certain personnel and medical files, trade secrets, internal memoranda, police investigatory files, financial institutions and geological and geophysical information. The right of access to records was improved by amendments in 1974 which set times limits for agency response, allow recovery of legal fees to a successful plaintiff, make possible the suspension of an employee who arbitrarily withholds information, and which allow a federal judge to review in private classified material to determine the legitimacy of the claim to necessary secrecy. The FOI Act requires the agency to justify not releasing the record rather than the citizen or reporter having to justify why the record should be released.

**Freedom to Travel.** See Passport.

**Gag Order.** A label applying both to formal prior restraint by injunction and to court orders commanding prosecution and defense attorneys and other trial participants not to give information to the press beyond whatever is on the court record. The latter gag order is more prevalent than the first.

**Good Motives and Justifiable Ends.** The basic defense of truth in civil libel is modified in some states by the added requirement that the truth must be published with good motives and for justifiable ends. One line of reasoning behind the added phrase is that it gives a person rehabilitated from an old crime some defense against the republication of the old record. The news medium would have to justify the republication by something more than the mere truth of the original record. In criminal libel, the constitutions of 18 states add the same phrase to the defense of truth.

**Grand Jury.** A group of citizens who decide whether the evidence presented to it justifies an indictment, that is, an accusation of a capital or other serious crime. U.S. Supreme Court Justice Byron R. White in *Branzburg v. Hayes,* where the issue was whether reporters could be compelled to testify before grand juries, describes it this way: ''Grand jury proceedings are constitutionally mandated for capital or other serious crimes and 'its constitutional prerogatives are rooted in long centuries of Anglo-American history' . . . . Because its task is to inquire into the existence of criminal conduct and to return only well-founded indictments, its investigative powers are necessarily broad.'' A trial jury (petit jury) decides guilt or innocence. A grand jury indicts or finds no cause for action. Its deliberations are secret. At its best, it protects citizens against overzealous prosecutors, but critics charge that its secrecy lends itself to abuse of witnesses and to manipulation by prosecutors. In the federal system, all felony prosecutions are initiated by a grand jury indictment unless that right is waived, in which case the felony case is begun by an information (specific charges of wrongdoing as in an indictment but issued by a prosecutor). In state prosecutions of felonies, the respondent (defendant) does not have the same right to grand jury review and action unless the state law requires it.

**Graphic Work (Copyright).** See Pictorial Work.

**Gravamen.** The central point of a claim or an accusation, the essence of the issue. U.S. Supreme Court Justice Byron R. White explained it in *Cox Broadcasting v. Cohn*: "Because the gravamen of the claimed injury is the publication of information, whether true or not, the dissemination of which is embarrassing or otherwise painful to an individual, it is here that the claims of privacy most directly confront the Constitution."

# h

**Habeas Corpus.** Habeas is from the Latin habere (to have). Corpus is Latin for body. It is a writ whereby a judge orders anyone holding anyone else in custody (e.g. a sheriff holding a prisoner) to come before the court and justify the custody. Habeas corpus historically is the writ whereby the judiciary protects the citizen against exeutive tyranny. It is therefore an enormously important power, a writ of freedom so to speak. Not usually involved in media law questions, one instance where it was involved is *Sheppard v. Maxwell,* which begins, "This federal habeas corpus application involves the question whether Sheppard was deprived of a fair trial...." Sheppard was in the Ohio penitentiary and argued that he was improperly in custody because his trial for the murder of his wife was prejudiced by media.

**Hostile Audience.** If an audience is hostile to a speaker, should the police stop the speaker in order to defuse the audience or should the audience be stopped, perhaps by threat of arrest, from interfering with the speaker's right to speak? And should a speaker be barred by court order from speaking at all because his identity and previously-stated positions are known to be inflammatory? The N.Y. Appellate Court gave this guideline in *Rockwell v. Morris,* a case involving George Lincoln Rockwell, an American Nazi, and a proposed appearance in a New York City park. Ruling that a permit should be granted, the high court said: "A community need not wait to be subverted by street riots and storm troopers; but also, it cannot . . . suppress a speaker, in prior restraint, on the basis of news reports, hysteria or inference that what he did yesterday, he will do today." But if he "incites others to immediate unlawful action he may be punished." Such incitement, however, "is not to be confused with unlawful action" by the audience seeking to suppress the speaker. The court went on, "the unpopularity of views, their shocking quality, their obnoxiousness and even their alarming impact is not enough. Otherwise . . . the anti-racist himself could be suppressed, if he undertakes to speak in restricted areas; and one who asks that public schools be opened indiscriminately to all ethnic groups could be lawfully suppressed, if only he chose to speak where persuasion is most needed." See Fighting Words.

**Hot Line.** As a convenience to media, some police departments use a special telephone connection to report to media outlets the essential facts of breaking crime stories. The message is composed by a police officer or other police department employee. Errors in a "hot line" report are not protected by the qualified privilege found in common law to report official proceedings, according to a case in the District of Columbia. Therein, the court distinguished between offical police records of arrests and the "hot line" which did not "carry the dignity and authoritative weight as a record for which the common law sought to provide a reporting privilege" because the hot line is "nothing more sanctified than unofficial statements of police regarding a crime." The court pointed out, however, that the ruling did not preclude the newspaper "from showing that its reliance on the hot line report was reasonable and thus avoid liability." *Phillips v. Evening Star Newspaper.*

**House Organ.** It is doubtful under present case law that house organs have the same privileges under the First Amendment as the standard commercial press. They are more likely to be seen as a captive publication, a part of the general business enterprise of the sponsoring company. This affects some aspects of copy handling. For example, some companies require release forms for all pictures in the house organ identifying an individual, whereas pictures in standard newspapers or broadcasting are more likely to be covered by "newsworthiness" as a protection against privacy-invasion suits. Manifestly, some articles in house organs are of general public interest, but articles which are more in the nature of product or company promotion and magazines dominated by such articles are likely to be judged under First Amendment standards less broad than mass media journalism enjoys.

# i

**Impact Theory.** This approach varies the interpretation of the First Amendment according to differentials in the impact of each medium on an audience. U.S. Supreme Court Justice Robert H. Jackson, concurring in *Kovacs v. Cooper* that an ordinance was constitutional which curtailed "loud and raucous" noises by a sound truck, expressed it this way. "The moving picture screen, the radio, the newspaper, the handbill, the sound truck and the street corner orator have differing natures, values, abuses and dangers. Each in my view is a law unto itself. . . ." And in dissent in *Kunz v. New York,* Justice Jackson said: "The vulnerability of various forms of communication to community control must be proportioned to their impact upon other community interests." Some inference of the same reasoning lies in the unwillingness of the U.S. Supreme Court to grant motion pictures the same freedom as freedom of the press. See Motion Pictures. And Justice Byron R. White, for the majority in *Red Lion Broadcasting v. FCC,* stated: "Although broadcasting is clearly a medium affected by a First Amendment interest, differences in the characteristics of new media justify differences in the First Amendment standards applied to them." Against this impact theory is the argument that since the constitution protects freedom of speech and of the press without reference to form of delivery, each medium should be treated the same under it, a view held by Justice Hugo L. Black who read the First Amendment in *Kovacs* as covering "all present instruments of communication, as well as others that inventive genius may bring into being."

**Imprimatur.** Approved for publication. It means that the material meets the criteria for publication of the government or of the group from which permission to publish is sought. In books dealing with doctrines of the Catholic Church, it is usually joined with *nihil obstat* (nothing objectionable), meaning that the material is doctrinally accurate and not misleading.

**In Camera.** In private. Refers to a judge holding a hearing or examining documents privately, the public and press excluded.

**Incidental Restriction Doctrine.** Some small, indirect restriction on freedom of expression is constitutional if the restriction flows from legislation dealing with other valid interests of government. *United States v. O'Brien,* a case involving "symbolic speech," i.e. draft card burning, defines this doctrine. An incidental restriction is justified "if it is within the constitutional power of the government; if it furthers an important or substantial governmental interest; if the governmental interest is unrelated to the suppression of free expression; and if the incidental restriction on alleged First Amendment freedoms is no greater than is essential to the furtherance of that interest." Under this doctrine, the U.S. Supreme Court upheld a Detroit zoning ordinance restricting the location of adult bookstores and motion picture houses. *Young v. American Mini Theatres.*

**Incitement.** One attempt to distinguish advocacy from incitement, the former permitted under the First Amendment, the latter not, is whether the words used are aimed at producing "imminent lawless action." The U.S. Supreme Court in *Brandenburg v. Ohio,* using affirmatively that distinction from another case, overturned Ohio's Criminal Syndicalism Act because it "purports to punish mere advocacy and to forbid, on pain of criminal punishment, assembly with others merely to advocate . . ." criminal syndicalism, i.e. advocating or teaching violence as a means of political or industrial reform. See Syndicalism Laws.

**Indecent Language (Broadcasting).** Federal law makes it a crime to broadcast "any obscene, indecent, or profane language." *18 U.S.C. Section 1464.* In 1973, WBAI-FM, New York, broadcast a recording by social satirist George Carlin using seven words common to street vocabulary to illustrate "words that you can't say" on public airwaves. On complaint of a father that the words came over his car radio while driving with his young son, the Federal Communications Commission reprimanded the station and issued an order forbidding the broadcasting of such words at program times when children would likely be in the audience. The FCC distinguished "obscene" from "indecent" language in that the former lacked an element necessary to obscenity—an "appeal to prurient interests." The U.S. Court of Appeals ruled that the FCC's action was censorship, calling the order "overbroad and vague" and likening it to "burning the house to roast the pig." The court said: "We should continue to trust the licensee to exercise judgment, responsibility, and sensitivity to the community's needs, interests and tastes. To whatever extend we err, or the Commission errs in balancing its duties, it must be in favor of balancing the values of free expression and freedom from governmental inter-

# i

ference in matters of taste." *Pacifica Foundation v. FCC.* A concurring opinion by a second of the three judges making the majority, argued that the FCC action did more than violate the statutory ban on FCC censorship, that it violated the First Amendment as well. The U.S. Supreme Court disagreed and held that the FCC order was a valid exercise of its authority. Justice John P. Stevens for the 5-4 majority wrote that "patently offensive, indecent material presented over the airwaves confronts the citizen, not only in public, but also in the privacy of the home, where the individual's right to be let alone plainly outweights the First Amendment rights of an intruder." And in relation to the "pig" imagery of the Appeals Court decision, Justice Stevens said, "we simply hold that when the Commission finds that the pig has entered the parlor, the exercise of its regulatory power does not depend on proof that the pig is obscene." Justice William J. Brennan, Jr., in dissent, said the majority view could "support the suppression of a good deal of political speech, such as the Nixon tapes and . . . could even provide the basis for imposing sanctions for the broadcast of certain portions of the Bible." *FCC v. Pacifica Foundation, No. 77-528, (July 3, 1978).*

**Infringement.** Copying material from a copyrighted work without permission of the owner of the copyright is an infringement of copyright and punishable (unless the material used is covered by fair use). Infringement suits generally require the copyright owner to prove that the alleged infringer had access to the copyrighted work and did copy it, substantial similarity being one of the tests of copying. If the defendant can prove that his work is original with him, he can overcome the infringement suit.

**Injunction.** A writ issued by a judge ordering someone to refrain from an action or to stop an action underway. Prior restraint on media in its most direct meaning takes place when a court issues an injunction ordering news or comment not to be printed or broadcast. Such injunctions are presumptively invalid. The First Amendment requires a heavy burden of proof that the injunction is necessary. See Prior Restraint.

**Injuria Verbalis.** In Roman law, oral defamation or slander; distinct from famosus libellus, which is written defamation or libel.

**Inter Alia.** Among other things. Used in quoting part of a statute or a decision to indicate that the part mentioned is only one of several items dealt with in the quoted source.

**Interlocutory Order.** A temporary or provisional order within a law suit, subject to change when the case as a whole is decided.

**Intrusion.** One form of invasion of privacy. It includes bugging, wiretapping, snooping through windows and overzealous shadowing. "Unlike other types of invasion of privacy, intrusion does not involve as one of its essential elements the publication of the information obtained. The tort is complete with the obtaining of the information by improperly intrusive means." *Pearson v. Dodd*. In that case, the U.S. Court of Appeals, District of Columbia Circuit, added, "we approve the extension of the tort of invasion of privacy to instances of intrusion, whether by physical trespass or not, into spheres from which an ordinary man in a plaintiff's position could reasonably expect that the particular defendant would be excluded." The court, however, held Washington columnist Drew Pearson not liable because in "an untried and developing area of tort law, we are not prepared to go so far" as to ". . . establish the proposition that one who receives information from an intruder, knowing it has been obtained by improper intrusion, is guilty of a tort."

**Investment Adviser.** A person who for compensation advises others orally or in writing about buying or selling securities. An investment adviser must register with the U.S. Securities and Exchange Commission. The applicable statute, however, specifically excludes "the publisher of any bona fide newspaper" of general circulation.

# j

**Joint Operating Agreement.** The combining under one corporation of production, distribution and business office functions of two newspapers in the same town while maintaining separate editorial identities. Such agreements are permitted under the 1970 federal Newspaper Preservation Act.

**Joint Work (Copyright).** A work prepared by two or more authors with the intention that their contributions be merged into inseparable or interdependent parts of a unitary whole.

**Judicial Gloss.** The accumulation of decisions and reasonings on a particular statute or constitutional point. The sense of the phrase is expressed in *Miami Herald v. Tornillo,* wherein the U.S. Supreme Court says that if the issue is governmental coercion of a newspaper, "this at once brings about a confrontation with the express provisions of the First Amendment and the judicial gloss on that amendment developed over the years."

**Juvenile Offenders.** Juvenile court records and hearings are usually not public. The U.S. Supreme Court has upheld the right of a state "to provide and to improve provision for the confidentiality of records of police contacts and court actions relating to juveniles." *In re Gault.* The counter views of courts and journalism were well summarized in *Oklahoma Publishing Co. v. District Court.* "The argument for requiring juvenile proceedings to be confidential is that: exposure of a juvenile's record of delinquency would be likely to cause impairment of rehabilitative goals . . . cause the juvenile offender to lose employment opportunities . . . bring undue humiliation upon his family . . . and that publicity may afford the hard core delinquent the kind of recognition he desires. The argument for freedom of the press to report juvenile proceedings is that the press is the watchdog of society and that if they are precluded by statute from reporting a matter of public interest, soon any judicial proceeding could be made subject to private proceedings, and a return to the star chamber would inure as a direct result of denial of the right of the press to unrestrainedly gather the news."

# k

**Katzenbach Rules.** A set of guidelines formulated by U.S. Attorney General Nicholas deB. Katzenbach to govern the release of potentially prejudicial information by federal law enforcement officials. Released in April 1965, the rules generally are the same as free press—fair trial guildelines voluntarily agreed to by press and bar groups in various states: no conclusionary statements as to guilt or innocence, no volunteering information about a prior criminal record, about confessions, admissions or alibis, about fingerprints, polygraph examinations, ballistic or other laboratory tests. "Disclosures should include only incontrovertible, factual matters, and should not include subjective observations," the guidelines state. Approved for release are the defendants name, age, residence, employment, marital status "and similar background information;" the charge, and the circumstances surrounding the arrest—time, place, resistance, pursuit if any, weapons used and items seized at the time of arrest. Two generalized exceptions were included: 1. if "the fair administration of justice" required release of information beyond the guidelines, the law enforcement official would have to have specific permission from Washington, and 2. "This statement of policy is not intended to restrict the release of information concerning a defendant who is a fugitive from justice"—an inferential admission that publicity can sometimes be helpful in catching criminals at large. *28 C.F.R. Section 50.2.*

# L

**Landmark Case.** A term usually reserved to U.S. Supreme Court decisions which firmly establish either new interpretations of the First Amendment or other constitutional questions or which answer constitutional questions of great public policy significance. Hindsight is helpful in determining which cases are landmarks. In media law, *New York Times v. Sullivan* (libel), *Near v. Minnesota* (prior restraint), and *Roth v. United States* (obscenity), are samples of landmark decisions.

**LAPS Test.** An acronym for a description of protected expression. "At a minimum, prurient, patently offensive depiction or description of sexual conduct must have serious literary, artistic, political, or scientific value to merit First Amendment protection." *Miller v. California.*

**Lascivious.** Something is lascivious if it tends to excite lust or undermine morals regarding sexual relations. In *Roth v. United States,* the trial judge told the jury: "The words 'obscene, lewd and lascivious' as used in the law, signify that form of immorality which has relation to sexual impurity and has a tendency to excite lustful thoughts."

**Law.** Binding rules of conduct and relationship imposed by society upon its members and enforceable through sanctions for violations thereof. See Common Law, Natural Law, Statutory Law.

**Leapfrogging.** Occurs when cable television imports a distant signal over the signal of closer stations. The fear that cable would select from stations in New York, Chicago or Los Angeles to the competitive disadvantage of closer stations led to an FCC rule which required to give priority to the two nearest of the top 25 markets. Cable systems authorized to carry a third independent UHF station could reach up to 200 miles for it; and where exclusivity protection came into play, the point of origin of substitute material could be ignored. The FCC dropped the rule in 1976.

**Legal Advertising.** A wide range of activities by government are required to be published in a newspaper as a form of notice to the public. These include such actions as notices of bankruptcy, sale of public property, bids for public contracts, offerings of bonds, sale of land for delinquent taxes, special assessments (the list varies in different states). In some states, notice by radio and television is also acceptable. Also called public notice advertising, it is a significant source of income for smaller newspapers particularly.

**Legislate Morality.** Controls on pornography are sometimes criticized as an attempt to legislate morality, the argument being that moral judgments belong to individual discretion and are not a proper area for government intrusion. The Eighteenth Amendment, ratified in 1919 and repealed in 1933, which banned intoxicating liquors, is frequently used as an example of the futility of legislating a moral choice. The phrase is appealing but the idea is shallow. Law deals with many questions which have moral roots—murder, for example. Law also affects what is morally acceptable in society. For example, civil rights laws do not of themselves change individual moral attitudes but they operate to make bigotry socially unacceptable and to punish actions following from it.

**Letter of Compliance.** An informal agreement between the Federal Trade Commission and an advertiser that some advertising practices be stopped. It is not an admission of guilt that the advertising was deceptive. It represents essentially a negotiated agreement to change some practice which the FTC staff finds undesirable. A similar practice in the Federal Communications Commission is sometimes called regulation by "raised eyebrow."

**Lewd.** In early English usage, it meant rudeness, coarseness, vulgarity. In obscenity rulings today, it's commonly used as a synonym for lasciviousness.

**Liability Without Fault.** Time was when "you publish at your peril" was the prevalent doctrine in libel, meaning liability regardless of any fault in the sense of culpable negligence on the part of the publication. This is the common law libel standard of strict liability. The doctrine has been modified to require a showing of actual malice in libel of public persons and a showing of some fault in libel of private citizens. "We hold that, as long as they do not impose liability without fault, the states may define for themselves the appropriate standard of liability for a publisher or broadcaster of a defamatory falsehood injurious to a private individual." *Gertz v. Welch.* Like local community standards in obscenity, standards of liability under this decision need not be identical among the states, creating thereby a potential unevenness in libel verdicts and an unsureness in media.

**Libel.** Defamation in any form of expression more permanent than mere speech. Whether defamation broadcast is libel or slander depends on state precedents and the particular facts, but the tendency in law is to regard broadcast defamation as libel because its reach is broad and it frequently has the "permanency" of a script or tape.

**Libel—Civil.** The defaming of one person by another. Civil libel is the most common form of libel in the United States, criminal libel having been diminished, if not eliminated, by court decisions. The theory underlying libel is that each person has a right to a good reputation, to acceptance in the community. Defamation damages reputation and is therefore actionable in law by a suit for damages. Libel of private citizens is distinguished in law from libel of public persons, the latter requiring a different burden of proof through application of the New York Times rule. Libel is per se if the defamation is obvious on the face of it, e.g. false or unprivileged accusations of a crime, of mental disorder, of lack of chastity particularly in a woman, of lack of fitness in a job or profession. Libel per quod is defamation by circumstances surrounding the story which may not be apparent through the story itself. Thus, to say someone got married yesterday might be defamatory if he or she were already married since the story then implies bigamy. The defenses against a libel action are truth, fair comment and its extension in the New York Times rule, or privilege i.e. the qualified privilege to report news from privileged sources.

**Libel—Criminal.** Historically, words defamatory of government have been punishable as sedition, a form of criminal libel. Defamation of an individual could also be prosecuted as a crime. The theory behind sedition is that government needs the respect of the people in order to govern and that words defamatory of government disturb the public tranquility in ways that could lead to a breach of the peace. Similarly, defaming an individual might provoke him to breach the peace. The libeller should be prosecuted because his words created the provocation. Criminal libel in early American history and in British history before that operated as a weapon of suppression. Truth was not in itself a defense since the greater the truth the greater the potential damage to government or likelihood of provoking discord. Many state constitutions now say that truth is a defense if joined with "good motives and justifiable ends." The additional qualification on truth is not constitutional in regard to a criminal libel charge brought by a public official. *Garrison v. Louisiana.* And in 1976 a California criminal libel law was ruled unconstitutional for the same language in a prosecution on behalf of an actress who sought criminal punishment against a publication for using her face on the body of an unidentified nude. The validity of criminal libel today under any circumstances is so doubtful that media no longer consider it a threat.

**Libel—Damages.** Compensatory damages, also called general or presumed, are the damages assumed to exist in libel per se without proof of damages. The libel being clear and unarguable, the plaintiff is entitled to some money (providing, of course, that the libel is not overcome by an aceptable defense). Actual damages are damages specifically alleged and proven—loss of wages or of customers for example. Libel per quod requires proof of actual damages. Punitive damages are a punishment to deter the libeller or others from similar libels in the future. The application of these traditional terms of damage in libel is affected by *Gertz v. Welch.* Under that ruling, punitive damages require a showing of actual malice. Compensatory damages, but not punitive damages, can be awarded private citizens if the publisher or broadcaster is guilty of a state-defined standard of fault, and actual damages can include compensation for personal humiliation, mental anguish and suffering.

**Libel—Group.** Libel of a class of citizens, classified by race, color, creed or religion, was sustained as constitutionally acceptable criminal libel by the U.S. Supreme Court in a case arising out of an Illinois statute. The court by 5-4 ruled it was a proper exercise of state power for Illinois ''to curb false or malicious defamation of racial and religious groups made in public places and by means calculated to have a powerful emotional impact on those to whom it was presented.'' The material from which the prosecution arose was against blacks and depicted them as depraved and as criminals. The opinion written by Justice Felix Frankfurter drew stinging dissents. Justice Hugo L. Black, for example, believed the law to be a gross violation of the First Amendment. He warned ''minority groups who hail this holding as their victory'' that '' . . . the same kind of state law that makes Beauharnais a criminal for advocating segregation in Illinois can be utilized to send people to jail in other states for advocating equality and nonsegregation.'' *Beauharnais v. Illinois.* No similar case has been heard since by the U.S. Supreme Court. And the Illinois statute

# L

at issue was subsequently repealed. Whether this concept of criminal libel would be upheld again is doubtful.

**Libel on Government.** A unit of government cannot be civilly libeled. Chicago, as a municipality, sued the Chicago Tribune for alleged defamation of the city in articles which asserted that the city was in perilous financial condition through mismanagement. The court ruled that "every citizen has a right to criticize an inefficient or corrupt government without fear of civil as well as criminal prosecution." Stating that the newspaper had admitted publishing "malicious and false statements regarding the city of Chicago with intent to destroy its credit and financial standing," the court held that "it is better that an occasional individual or newspaper that is so perverted in judgment and so misguided in his or its civic duty should go free, than that all of the citizens should be put in jeopardy of imprisonment or economic subjugation if they venture to criticize an inefficient or corrupt government." *City of Chicago v. Tribune Co.*

**Libel per quod, per se.** See Libel—Civil.

**Libel—Small Group.** What number constitutes a small group is not precisely determinable. If the group is "large", a libel of the group does not apply to individual members of the group, absent some more particular identification of someone within the group. If the group is small, cohesive, its membership easily known, the danger of applying a group libel to each member increases. In an alleged libel of saleswomen in a department store, the group (382) was held too large for individual suits, but individual suits by salesmen (25) in the same alleged libel were accepted. *Neiman-Marcus Co. v. Lait.*

**Licensee Qualifications.** Under Federal Communications Commission rules, the licensee must be a citizen, of good character, financially positioned to operate for one year without revenue, have or have access to the engineering competence required for broadcasting, and be within the limits of permissible ownership of other stations or of stations and newspapers.

**Licentious.** Now usually a synonym for obscenity. In the 16th and 17th centuries, the word more often described seditious language, grossly intemperate criticism or action unrestrained by law or morality. References to the "licentious press" appear frequently in early writ-

# L

ings to describe a line beyond which the writer believed tolerance of press freedom should cease.

**Literary Works (Copyright).** Works, other than audiovisual works, expressed in words, numbers, or other verbal or numerical symbols or indicia, regardless of the nature of the material objects, such as books, periodicals, manuscripts, phonorecords, film, tapes, disks, or cards, in which they are embodied.

**Little Merchant Plan.** Under this arrangement, the newspaper delivery boy or girl is considered to be an independent contractor rather than an employee of the newspaper. The distinction affects many legal questions, e.g. minimum wages, social security and withholding taxes and labor standards regulations.

**Local Service Area—Primary Transmitter.** For television, the area in which the Federal Communications Commission rules apply to retransmission of the station's signal by a cable system. For radio, it's the primary service area, which means "the area in which the ground wave is not subject to objectionable interference or objectionable fading." *Title 47 C.F.F. Section 73.11 (a).*

**Long-Arm Statute.** A person in Wyoming alleged that he had been defamed by an article in a California newspaper on the subject of organized crime in Wyoming. The story was researched in Wyoming and carried a Wyoming dateline. The newspaper asserted that it had no news service subscribers in Wyoming. The long-arm law came into play in deciding which federal district court had jurisdiction in the libel suit. The Wyoming statute covers anyone outside a state causing "tortious injury" within the state. Libel suits are tort actions. The U.S. Court of Appeals, Tenth Circuit, held that the federal district court in Wyoming had jurisdiction. The U.S. Supreme Court refused to review. The applicable law then becomes Wyoming law under a diversity action (which see). *Anselmi v. Denver Post.* (The Denver Post was included in the suit but the long-arm statute question was raised by the California newspaper). Most states have long-arm statutes. Essentially, they are procedural laws which give a state jurisdiction over a person based on actions by that person within the state or contacts the person has had within the state. Federal courts look to state long-arm statutes to determine jurisdictional aspects of federal civil actions.

# L

**Lottery.** Three elements are necessary to make a lottery. "The distribution of prizes according to chance for a consideration." *FCC v. American Broadcasting Co.* Chance means generally that skill or judgment are not more dominant than simple luck in determining the winner. Consideration means that something of value is required to enter the contest, e.g. purchase of a product or the expenditure of considerable time and effort. If any of the three elements is lacking, it's not a lottery. In 1975, in recognition of the growth of government-operated lotteries in several states, a federal law was passed which allows radio and television stations in such states to broadcast lottery information and advertisements, and stations in adjacent states can also broadcast such material on the neighboring state's lottery. Further, the statute permits newspapers published in lottery states to publish lottery information in editions mailed to subscribers, but newspapers are still prohibited from carrying information on another state's lottery in mail editions.

**Loudspeakers.** It's unconstitutional for a municipal ordinance to give "uncontrolled discretion" to the chief of police, or any other functionary, to regulate sound trucks. "Loud-speakers are today indispensible instruments of effective public speech. The sound truck has become an accepted method of political campaigning. It is the way people are reached." And "noise can be regulated by regulating decibels. The hours and place of public discussion can be controlled. But to allow the police to bar the use of loud-speakers because their use can be abused is like barring radio receivers because they too can make a noise." *Sais v. New York.* "We think it is a permissible exercise of legislative discretion to bar sound trucks with broadcasts of public interest, amplified to a loud and racuous volume, from the public ways of municipalities." And "opportunity to gain the public's ears by objectionably amplified sound on the streets is no more assured by the right of free speech than is the unlimited opportunity to address gatherings on the streets. The preferred position of freedom of speech in a society that cherishes liberty for all does not require legislators to be insensible to claims by citizens to comfort and convenience." *Kovacs v. Cooper.*

**Lowest Unit Rate.** A requirement imposed by Congress in 1971 on licensed media that the rate for political advertising be not higher than the unit charge for the commercial advertiser most favored in a quantity discount. The requirement applies for 45 days before a primary election and 60 days before a general or special election. In effect, it gives political candidates (but not spokespersons for them) the benefit of quantity discounts allowed long-term commercial advertisers.

**Magna Carta.** In June of 1215, the English barons forced King John to grant them certain civil and political liberties. The granting document is the Magna Carta or Great Charter. It is unrelated to freedom of expression except in the tenuous sense that the Magna Carta represents a beginning from which to trace a decline in the absolute power of the monarchy and a growth in British freedoms generally.

**Malice—Actual.** The First Amendment "prohibits a public official from recovering damages for a defamatory falsehood relating to his official conduct unless he proves that the statement was made with 'actual malice'—that is, with knowledge that it was false or with reckless disregard of whether it was false or not." *New York Times v. Sullivan.* Four years later in 1968, the Supreme Court said: " . . . reckless conduct is not measured by whether a reasonably prudent man would have published or would have investigated before publishing. There must be sufficient evidence to permit the conclusion that the defendant in fact entertained serious doubts as to the truth of his publication. Publishing with such doubts shows reckless disregard for truth or falsity and demonstrates actual malice." *St. Amant v. Thompson* Other cases say that a "high degree of awareness of probable falsity" is required for actual malice.

**Malice—Common Law.** Intentionally doing something wrong without sufficient cause or excuse. In libel or slander, it connotes ill-will, desire to harm, rancor, spite, wantonness. Whether any of its several shadings of meaning apply depends on the facts in the particular case. Malice in the sense of evil motive can undermine the defenses of fair comment and privilege.

**Marketplace of Ideas.** The idea that citizens in a democracy are well served if opinions of all kinds, accurate or inaccurate, are freely circulated is summarized in this phrase. The metaphor is borrowed from classical economics wherein the marketplace would determine the quality and distribution of goods if the market were free of controls by government or monopolists. In a free marktplace of ideas, error is tolerated because truth will emerge from the clash of differing opinions. Wide-open, uninhibited discourse should be encouraged, this theory holds; and the function of journalism through any media is to be sure the marketplace is well stocked with ideas for the people to choose among. "It is the purpose of the First Amendment to preserve an uninhibited marketplace of ideas in which truth will ultimately prevail . . . ." *Red Lion Broadcasting v. F.C.C.* The opposite of a free market is a market wherein public authority or private combinations of power select what goods or ideas are available. Some critics of the marketplace metaphor say that some enforceable right of access to print media is necessary to make the marketplace work. Others argue that misleading ideas like misleading advertising of products need controlling because years may go by before truth catches up with error.

**Marking of Advertising Matter.** "Editorial or other reading matter contained in publications entered as second class mail and for the publication of which a valuable consideration is paid, accepted or promised, shall be marked plainly 'advertisement' by the publisher." *Title 39 U.S.C.A. Section 4367.*

**Mass Media.** Media which regularly disseminate information of a general character to an undifferentiated audience, e.g. radio and television, daily and weekly newspapers, news and article magazines. The First Amendment also covers special audience media, e.g. a labor newspaper. House organs, publications whose reason for being is primarily enhancement of a business or public service enterprise, and private letters, may not have the same degree of First Amendment protection as mass media.

**Material and Substantial Interference.** A standard for judging the limits on freedom of expression by students in schools. In *Tinker v. Des Moines Community School District,* the U.S. Supreme Court expressed it this way (the case involved disciplining students for wearing arm bands to protest the Vietnam war): "In order for the state in the person of school officials to justify prohibition of a particular expression of opinion, it must be able to show that its action was caused by something more than a mere desire to avoid the discomfort and unpleasantness that always accompany an unpopular viewpoint. Certainly where there is . . . no showing that . . . the forbidden conduct would 'materially and substantially interfere with the requirements of appropriate discipline in the operation of the school,' the prohibition cannot be sustained."

# m

**Money.** Black and white printed illustrations of paper money, checks, bonds, and other obligations and securities of the United States and foreign governments are permitted for numismatic, historical, educational and newsworthy purposes, but not for general advertising (numismatic advertising, OK). No illustrations may be in color. The illustration must be less than three-fourths or more than one and one-half times the size of the genuine article. The illustration must relate to an accompanying story (merely decorative pictures are forbidden), and all plates, negatives and prints must be destroyed after their use. Motion picture films, microfilms and slides in black and white only are permitted for telecasting, entertainment or educational purposes.

**Most Susceptible Person Test.** In 1868, obscenity was defined in England as material which would "deprave and corrupt those whose minds are open to such immoral influences." *Regina v. Hicklin*. In other words, obscenity is judged by its influence on persons most likely to be adversely influenced by it. The test is also known as the Hicklin rule. See Average Person Test.

**Motion Pictures.** In 1915, the U.S. Supreme Court said movies were not included in the First Amendment. ". . . the exhibition of moving pictures is a business, pure and simple . . . not to be regarded . . . as part of the press of the country, or as organs of public opinion." *Mutual Film Corp. v. Industrial Commission of Ohio*. In 1952, the court put movies under the First Amendment. ". . . expression by means of motion pictures is included within the free speech and free press guaranty of the First and Fourteenth Amendments." *Burstyn v. Wilson*. In 1959, the court said it wasn't ready to decide whether freedom of expression in movies is "precisely co-extensive with . . . newspapers, books or individual speech." *Kingsley International Pictures v. New York*. In 1962, the court indicated that censorship of motion pictures for obscenity was possible if a censorship statute provided for a prompt judicial determination in an adversary hearing with the censor required to justify the censorship rather than the distributor to justify overturning the censor's ruling. In short, a state or city can constitutionally pre-screen movies but any censorship must have judicial approval before it's effective. *Freedman v. Maryland*.

**Motion Pictures (Copyright).** Audiovisual works consisting of a series of related images which, when shown in succession, impart an impression of motion, together with accompanying sounds, if any.

# m

**Motion Picture Ratings.** These are set by a seven-person Classification and Rating Administration, appointed with the approval of the president of the Motion Picture Association of America. Appeals from its decisions go to an appeals board of 23 members drawn from the MPA, theater owners and independent distributors. The ratings are: G— general audience, all ages admitted; PG—parental guidance suggested; R—restricted, those under 17 must be accompanied by a parent or adult guardian; X—no one under 17 admitted (age limit varies in some areas). No film maker is obliged to participate but since the members of the National Association of Theater Owners usually do not show unrated films, some pressure exists to submit to the rating board. The ratings themselves do not have any standing in media law. Some observers, however, see the system as a protection against periodic moves for formal movie censorship boards.

**Multiple Ownership Rule.** Under a Federal Communications Commission rule, one person can own no more than 7 AM radio stations, 7 FM radio stations and 7 television stations (5 VHF and 2 UHF), and in the same market, no more than one television, one AM, and one FM radio station.

**Multitude of Tongues.** Another way of expressing the idea that the public is well served by an uninhibited marketplace of ideas wherein speaking one's mind whether in abstract discussion or vigorous advocacy is encouraged. ". . . right conclusions are more likely to be gathered out of a multitude of tongues, than through any kind of authoritative selection. To many this is, and always will be folly; but we have staked upon it our all." *United States v. Associated Press.*

# n

**National News Council.** Founded in 1973 and funded by a consortium of foundations, this 18-member group (a mix of journalists and public representatives) monitors press performance by investigating complaints and issuing findings of exoneration or fault as the issue warrants. Its findings have no legal status but constitute in the aggregate a body of opinions on ethical performance by media. Complaints are screened by the council's staff to eliminate those *prima facie* without merit. Of 250 cases in the first year, 44 were deemed worth further investigation and 4 complaints (of the 44) were upheld by the council. Some news outlets oppose the idea as "meddling" by an outside group into individual editorial freedom. The council has gained considerable acceptance, however, on the basis of its performance. Similar national councils exist in Britain and Sweden. The council's address is One Lincoln Plaza, New York, N.Y. 10023.

**National Security.** To justify restraining publication on the grounds of national security requires the same heavy burden of proof required in any instance of prior restraint by injunction. In *New York Times v. United States,* the U.S. Supreme Court ruled per curiam that the federal government had failed to prove a jeopardy sufficient to continue the injunction against that newspaper printing the Pentagon Papers. The case evoked nine separate opinions. Justice Hugo L. Black argued that the government was making a ". . . bold and dangerously far-reaching contention that the courts should take it upon themselves to 'make' a law abridging freedom of the press in the name of equity, presidential power and national security." He felt that "to find that the president has 'inherent power' to halt the publication of news by resort to the courts would wipe out the First Amendment . . . ." And, "the word 'security' is a broad, vague generality whose contours should not be invoked to abrogate . . . the First Amendment." Justice William J. Brennan, Jr., however, saw an inherent conflict between legitimate boundaries of national security and a free press. Concluding that the government had failed to prove "direct, immediate and irreparable damage" to national security, Justice Brennan said: "... it is clear to me that it is the constitutional duty of the executive—as a matter of sovereign prerogative and not as a matter of law as the courts know law—through . . . executive regulations, to protect the confidentiality necessary to carry out its responsibilities in the fields of international relations and national defense." Taken as a whole, the decision implied that a grave threat to national security would justify prior restraint.

**Natural Law.** A system of law, independent of statutory or common law, in which rights and duties are seen as inherent in the nature of any being simply as being. Natural law is seen as discernible to human intelligence by reasoning both inductive and deductive. Each being has a right to those things necessary to fulfill its nature. These inherent rights precede rights granted by government or society and ought not to be infringed by either. That individuals have "certain unalienable rights, that among these are life, liberty and the pursuit of happiness" is a doctrine rooted in natural law. Further, natural law argues that human beings, having the capacity to reason, are more than sentient animals and have a right by nature to freedom of expression and to information, both seen as necessary to human nature itself. Natural law began with the Stoics but is now identified with the Scholastic school of philosophy.

**Negligence.** William L. Prosser, an authority on torts, defines it as "behavior which should be recognized as involving unreasonable danger to others. It's not so much a question of intent as it is that a reasonable person would have anticipated the damage and would have guarded against it." One court defines it as "conduct which creates an unreasonable risk of harm . . . the failure to use that amount of care which a reasonably prudent person would use under like circumstances." *Peagler v. Phoenix Newspapers*. The word is important in libel because some negligence as defined in each state is required under *Gertz v. Welch* for a private citizen to collect damages. Obviously, descriptions like "reasonably prudent" and "unreasonable risk" are imprecise, but they are as close as words can come to defining the concept.

**Neutral Reportage.** A First Amendment privilege which protects "the accurate and disinterested reporting" of defamatory charges made by a prominent organization or person "regardless of the reporter's views regarding their validity." Reasoning that "what is newsworthy about such accusations is that they are made," the U.S. Court of Appeals, Second Circuit, described neutral reportage in this way: "The contours of the press's right of neutral reportage are, of course, defined by the principle which gives life to it. Literal accuracy is not a prerequisite: if we are to enjoy the blessings of a robust and unintimidated press, we must provide immunity from defamation suits where the journalist believes, reasonably and in good faith, that his report accurately conveys the charges made." *Edwards v. National Audubon Society.*

**New.** In an advisory opinion in 1967, the Federal Trade Commission said that advertising a product as "new" requires some substantial and significant change in the product. Mere altering of the package, for example, would not suffice. And after six months, the FTC would "be inclined to question" continued use of "new" in advertisements unless some contrary reasons were offered in a particular case. Bona fide test marketing of a product is excluded from the six months guideline.

**Newsman's (Woman's) Privilege.** The right of a reporter or editor to refuse to testify as to the source of information or to refuse to bring notes and outakes before a court, grand jury or legislative inquiry. There is no First Amendment right to claim such a privilege. Some states, but not the federal government, have laws giving this privilege but the laws vary in wording and in judicial readings of their force and effect. "In 1958, a newsgatherer asserted for the first time that the First Amendment exempted confidential information from public disclosure . . . but the claim was denied, and this argument has been almost uniformly rejected since then, although there are occasional dicta that, in circumstances not presented, a newsman might be excused. These courts have applied the presumption against the existence of an asserted testimonial privilege and have concluded that the First Amendment interest asserted by the newsman was outweighed by the general obligation of a citizen to appear before a grand jury or at trial, pursuant to a subpoena, and give what information he possesses" *Branzburg v. Hayes.* Media's argument, unaccepted by the court, was that forcing reporters to testify would scare off future confidential sources and that the process would make journalism into an investigative arm of government. In practice, the federal government follows a policy of not subpoening reporters unless the information sought is believed essential to the investigation and is not available from any non-press sources. See Shield Laws.

**Newspaper.** Statutory definitions of newspapers usually require a publication in the English language containing news of a general character, a bona fide subscription list, and continuity of publication at regular intervals for a stated time, say two years. Some statutes specifically include free circulation newspapers and newspapers devoted wholly or chiefly to publishing legal news. What is and is not a newspaper is important in relation to legal advertising, to shield laws which protect employees of "newspapers," to registration under the Investment Advisors Act. The Newspaper Preservation Act defines "newspaper publication" as "a publication produced on newsprint paper which is published in one or more issues weekly (including as one publication any daily newspaper or any Sunday newspaper published by the same owner in the same city, community, or metropolitan area), and in which a substantial portion of the content is devoted to the dissemination of news and editorial content."

**Newspaper Preservation Act.** A federal statute passed in 1970 which exempted from antitrust prosecution 44 daily newspapers in 22 cities which were run under joint operating agreements (production, circulation, advertising under a central operation) while maintaining independent editorial departments. The law was passed in response to a holding that one form of such joint operation violated antitrust. *Citizens Publishing Co. v. United States.* The court ruled that the joint operation in Tucson used price fixing, profit pooling and market control "to end any business or commercial competition between the two papers." The Newspaper Preservation Act in effect overturned the court's decision.

**Newsworthiness.** A defense against an invasion-of-privacy suit, the term involves a number of elements: the importance of the issue, the timeliness of the story, the public interest in the facts as against mere public curiosity, the degree of public identity of the persons named, the passage of time in relation to how recalls of past events are handled. News from public records has the highest acceptance as newsworthy. Cases are more mixed on the newsworthiness of identifying participants in long past events in a way detrimental to their present lives. As press-privacy conflicts grow, judges will more often be called on to decide newsworthiness, a judgment which journalism claims is the proper function of editors and not of judges. "For better or worse, editing is what editors are for; and editing is selection and choice of material." *Columbia Broadcasting System, Inc. v. Democratic National Committee.*

**New York Times. Rule.** For a public official to sue successfully for libel, he must prove that the publication of the libel fits the definition of "actual malice" as given by the U.S. Supreme Court in *New York Times v. Sullivan:* "...that is, with knowledge that it was false or with reckless disregard of whether it was false or not." Subsequent cases applied the same rule to libel suits by public figures.

**Nihil Obstat.** See Imprimatur.

**Noscitur A Sociis.** The meaning of a particular word among several in a statute can be known by the words with which it is associated. The U.S. Court of Appeals, Seventh Circuit, in *United States v. Simpson,* ruled that the word "indecent" required an appeal to prurient interest as does the word "obscene" because the words appear together in the federal statute banning "obscene, indecent, or profane language" from broadcasting. "The maxim of construction noscitur a sociis is not irrelevant" in determining meaning, the court said. It's a rather elaborate way of waying that words should be read in context.

**Nunc Pro Tunc.** This means "now for then." It describes an action with retroactive effect. Its usage is shown in *Gannett Company v. De Pasquale,* a case involving the closing of a pre-trial hearing. "Three days later, counsel for Gannett appeared and asked the county court to reconsider and vacate its ruling *nunc pro tunc.*"

**Obiter Dictum.** Obiter means by the way and dictum means a remark. It refers to remarks in a judicial decision which are not essential to the ruling but which enlarge on it by bringing in various supporting reasons. Obiter is frequently dropped and dictum (singular) or dicta (plural) is used alone. Material considered dicta is not considered as precedent for subsequent cases. Many times it is difficult to determine where material essential to the decision leaves off and dicta begins.

**Obloquy.** Blame, censure, detraction. One of the words used in defining defamation.

**Official Newspaper.** In some states, local units of government, by resolution, sometimes designate a newspaper as the "official newspaper" for the purpose of legal advertising. The label does not give the governmental unit any control over the content of the newspaper.

**Official Secrets Acts.** Several laws in Great Britain make it a crime to release government information to any person not authorized to receive it. Both the giver and receiver, journalists included, can be prosecuted. When enforced it is a strong inhibition on freedom of the press. In 1975, Senate Bill No. 1, a recodification of federal criminal law, contained language which journalists said would have the same effect in the United States. A 1978 version (Senate Bill 1437) eliminated some provisions obnoxious to media (e.g. federal punishment for publishing government documents without permission) but retained others considered by the Freedom of Information Committee of the American Society of Newspaper Editors to be "ominous" (e.g. permitting criminal prosecutions of government employees who supply "private" information to reporters).

**One-to-a-Market Rule.** A Federal Communications Commission rule prohibiting one licensee from owning more than one television, one AM, and one FM station in the same market. Markets under 10,000 population and multiple ownerships already existing before March, 1970, are exempted. The phrase is sometimes applied also to cross ownership.

**Opinion of the Court.** The decision of an appellate court and its reasoning. In broader usage, the decision and opinion of any court of

**O**

record. U.S. Supreme Court decisions being with "Mr. Justice Someone delivered the opinion of the court." Sometimes the opinion of the
court is the opinion of a plurality rather than a majority, four justices
agreeing on the opinion but one or more other justices agreeing with
the ruling but not with the reasoning. The more the number of agreeing
justices, up to a unanimous agreement of the nine justices, the more
likely it is that the decision will stand in future similar media cases,
but later Supreme Courts can have a change of mind.

**Opprobrium.** The disgrace which is presumed to be attached to shame-
ful conduct. Hence, opprobrium is one of several words used in defining defamation to indicate that a serious damage to reputation
occurs when a person is defamed.

**Originality (Copyright).** Works to be copyrighted must be original. Originality does not mean literary skill, artistic value, novelty or clever-
ness, but rather only that the work was originated by the author.

**Orthodoxy.** Conformance to prevailing social or political beliefs or to the
tenets of a religious creed or particular political philosophy. The
First Amendment stands against punishment for unorthodox belief or
statements. "If there is any fixed star in our constitutional constel-
lation it is that no official, high or petty, can prescribe what shall be
orthodox in politics, nationalism, religion, or other matters of opinion
or force citizens to confess by word or act their faith therein. If there
are any circumstances which permit an exception, they do not now
occur to us." *West Virginia State Board of Education v. Barnette.*

**Overbreadth.** A statute drawn to punish expression not protected by the
First Amendment is unconstitutional if its reach infringes on protected expression. The remedy for overbreadth is a more precisely
written statute. Obviously it's not easy to distinguish between an unconstitutional overbreadth and a constitutional "incidental restriction."

**Owner (Copyright).** The person who owns any one of or all of the exclusive rights comprised in a copyright.

**Pandering.** A panderer is a go-between for procurement of sexual vice. Pandering is a concept in obscenity law which relates to the style and agressiveness of the display or advertising of obscene matter. It was made an element in judging obscenity in *Ginzburg v. United States,* where the court found the "leer of the sensualist" permeated the advertising of Ginzburg's material. The court said this was "the sordid business of pandering." Pandering is the commercial exploitation of prurient matter.

**Pandering Advertising Act.** A 1968 federal law which gives a receiver of advertising through the mail the right to declare on a postal form that the advertisement is obscene in his or her eyes, whereon the post office notifies the sender who then faces possible punishment if the material is again mailed to the complaining receiver. The U.S. Supreme Court upheld the law on the reasoning that the "mailer's right to communicate" stops at "the mailbox of an unreceptive addressee." The court rejected "categorically" the claim that the mailer had a constitutional right "to send unwanted material" to someone's home. *Rowan v. Post Office.*

**Parens Patriae.** "The power of the state through the court to act in the behalf of the child as a wise parent would." *Oklahoma Publishing v. District Court.*

**Passport.** The argument that a citizen has a First Amendment right to travel abroad in order to gather first-hand information on "the effects abroad of our government's policies, foreign and domestic, and with conditions abroad which might affect such policies" is not accepted by the U.S. Supreme Court. *Zemel v. Rusk.* The court said that authority to issue passports properly resides in the executive through the Passport Act of 1926 and a passport to Cuba could be denied for "considerations of national security." The court also said there was a constitutional right to travel within the United States—limited by government's right to quarantine an area "ravaged by flood, fire or pestilence." In a later case, the court turned down an argument that the First Amendment covered a right to receive information to a degree that made denial of a passport to a Belgian journalist, a

# p

Marxist, a violation of First Amendment rights. The journalist, Ernest Mandel, would have participated in seminars and other discussions in this country. Denying a passport to Mandel for a "facially legitimate and bona fide reason" within statutory authority did not infringe any First Amendment rights of Mandel's possible audiences. *Kleindienst v. Mandel.*

**Patent.** Copyright protects intellectual creations, ideas expressed in form (literature, music, paintings etc.). A patent protects ideas which embody inventiveness and are expressed in a machine, process or design. Copyrights are issued on compliance with proper notice of copyright. Patents are issued after a search of patents to see whether some previous patent is involved. Copyright is for the life of the author plus 50 years (as of 1978). Patents are for 17 years, no renewal. And "fair use" in copyright has no counterpart in patents.

**Per curiam.** An opinion of a court in which no individual judge or justice is identified as the author.

**Perform (Copyright).** To recite, render, play, dance, or act a work, either directly or by means of any device or process or, in the case of a motion picture or other audiovisual work, to show its images in any sequence or to make the sounds accompanying it audible.

**Periodical.** For purposes of second-class mail, a periodical "is a publication appearing at stated intervals, each number of which contains a variety of original articles by different authors, devoted either to general literature of some special branch of learning or to a special class of subjects." *Houghton v. Payne.* But the U.S. Court of Appeals, Third Circuit, in a recent case broadened the *Houghton* ruling: "...we think that the Postal Service must not be concerned with the originality of a periodical's literary content or a body count of its authors so much as with a nexus of the contents to periodicity, i.e. a recognized relationship between the various numbers and the continuity or connection between them." *Institute for Scientific Information v. Postal Service.* The ISI publication did not contain varied articles by different authors, but the court ruled in ISI's favor.

**Personal Attacks.** The Federal Communications Commission in July 1967, ordered: "When, during the presentation of views on a controversial issue of public importance, an attack is made upon the honesty, character, integrity or like personal qualities of an identified person or group, the licensee shall, within a reasonable time and in no event later than one week after the attack, transmit to the person or group attacked; 1. notification of the date, time and identification of the broadcast; 2. a script or tape (or an accurate summary if a script or tape is not available) of the attack; 3. an offer of a reasonable opportunity to respond over the licensee's facilities." Exempted are attacks by candidates or spokesmen therefor against other candidates or spokesmen, attacks on foreign groups or foreign public figures; and bona fide newscasts, interviews or on-the-spot news coverage. This personal attack rule was upheld by the U.S. Supreme Court against a claim that it violated the First Amendment. "Although broadcasting is clearly a medium affected by a First Amendment interest, differences in the characteristics of news media justify differences in the First Amendment standards applied to them," the opinion said. "There is nothing in the First Amendment which prevents the government from requiring a licensee to share his frequency with others and to conduct himself as a proxy or fiduciary with obligations to present those views and voices which are representative of his community and which would otherwise, by necessity, be barred from the airwaves." *Red Lion Broadcasting v. FCC.* There is no right to reply to an attack in print media.

**Person of Ordinary Sensibilities.** A guide phrase used in that form of invasion of privacy which deals with the publication of private facts. The Supreme Court of Alabama affirmed that standard in holding a newspaper liable for invasion of privacy for publishing a picture of a woman whose skirt was blown upwards by air jets in a fun house at a county fair. The court used as a judgment line whether the material would "outrage or cause mental suffering, shame or humiliation to a person of ordinary sensibilities." *Daily Times Democrat v. Graham.* Like the "average person" in obscenity, the phrase is not precisely definable but is used in a commonsense meaning.

**Pervasive Public Figure.** Persons who occupy positions of "persuasive power and influence" on public issues or who achieve "pervasive fame or notoriety" may become public figures for all purposes of media law, particularly libel and invasion of privacy actions. In *Gertz v. Welch,* the U.S. Supreme Court in setting forth those phrases went on, however, to say: "More commonly, an individual voluntarily injects himself or is drawn into a particular public controversy and thereby becomes a public figure for a limited range of issues." A person can, therefore, be a public figure yesterday and tomorrow but not

# p

today, depending on the circumstances. The person who injects himself or herself into a specific issue is called a vortex public figure and is a public figure only for that limited time and issue.

**Phonorecords (Copyright).** Material objects in which sounds, other than those accompanying a motion picture or other audiovisual work, are fixed by any method, and from which the sounds can be perceived, reproduced, or otherwise communicated, either directly or with the aid of a machine or device. The term includes the material object in which the sounds are first fixed.

**Pictorial Work (Copyright).** Pictorial, graphic and sculptural features that can be identified separately from, and are capable of existing independently of, the utilitarian aspects of the article.

**Piracy.** Unauthorized use of copyrighted materials. Piracy is used more often in relation to recordings and plagiarism is more commonly applied to the unauthorized use of literary material.

**Plagiarism.** Using someone's ideas or material as one's own. Plagiarism is avoided by giving full credit to the source. If the material is copyrighted, specific permission of the copyright owner is also required—except in situations covered by fair use.

**Plaintiff.** The person who initiates a lawsuit. The plaintiff in a criminal action is the public acting through a prosecutor. The plaintiff in a civil action is the person seeking redress from someone for some wrong. In state criminal actions, the plaintiff is referred to as the "state" and in federal criminal actions as the "government" or "United States."

**Pleadings.** The aggregate of documents filed by the parties during a lawsuit—complaint, response, discovery actions, etc. Jurisdictions differ on whether defamations in such pleadings are conditionally privileged for media use, that is reportable without jeopardy of libel if the report is fair and accurate. Jurisdictions against the privilege argue that a person could defame another through pleadings and then withdraw the suit after the defamation had been published "...the publication of accusations made by one party against another is neither a legal nor a moral duty of newspapers" and "To be safe, a newspaper has only to send its reporter to listen to hearings rather than to search the file of cases not yet brought before the court." *Sanford v. Boston Herald-Traveler.* In other words, no privilege attaches until the case is before the judge. A minority of jurisdictions agree with New York which allows the conditional privilege on the theory that the legal action has commenced when the pleadings are filed. *Campbell v. New York Evening Post.* Material in depositions is not privileged until the deposition is entered in the trial. Material in formal criminal accusations—indictments and informations—is privileged.

**Political Advertising.** Federal law states that "no person, association, organization, committee, or corporation shall publish or distribute or cause to be published or distributed any printed, multigraphed, photographed, typewritten, or written pamphlet, circular, card, dodger, poster, advertisement, or any other statement relating to or concerning, any candidate for election as president or vice-president, or senator or representative, in, or delegate or resident commissioner to, the Congress of the United States, unless such . . . contains the name or names . . . responsible for the publication or distribution of same . . ." States have similar laws requiring source identification for political advertising.

**Political Disclaimer.** Many states require that specific source identification be included in political advertising in print and broadcast media. Michigan's 1976 finance reporting act is an example. Any advertisement relating to an election, a candidate or a ballot question must contain a complete name and address of the person or committee paying for the advertisement, and if it is placed by a support group without the candidate's consent, the source identification must state also: "Not authorized by the candidate committee of John Doe." The identification/disclaimer must be clearly visible or audible.

**Political Editorials (Licensed Media).** The Federal Communications Commission ruled in July 1967, that: "Where a licensee, in an editorial, (i) endorses or (ii) opposes a legally qualified candidate or candidates, the licensee shall, within 24 hours after the editorial, transmit to respectively (i) the other qualified candidate or candidates for the same office or (ii) the candidate opposed in the editorial 1. notification of the date and the time of the editorial; 2. a script or tape of the editorial; and 3. an offer of a reasonable opportunity for a candidate to respond over the licensee's facilities." If the editorial is broadcast within 72 hours of election day, the licensee must notify the candidate far enough in advance to allow him to respond. Truth of falsity of the attack is not an element in this right to reply.

# p

**Political Season.** A calendar time specified by a legislature covering when a candidate for office can use paid advertising to advance his candidacy. In *Sadowski v. Shevin,* an appellate court in Florida held that limiting political advertising to a "political season" is unconstitutional because candidates had a First Amendment right to advocate issues and their candidacies through advertising.

**Pop-Up Advertisements.** The U.S. Postal Service defines these as die-cut pieces pasted to a folded sheet bound into or enclosed in publications which pieces, when the sheet is unfolded, assume a vertical position. For second-class mail privileges, publications must be printed sheets and "pop-ups" are not printed sheets.

**Pornography.** Generally a synonym for obscenity but now coming more to mean very explicit pictures or drawings of sexual activities. Obscenity still has some usage to describe sexually-oriented material not totally pornographic and is used also to describe something grossly offensive as in saying that war is obscene. Pornocracy means government by profligate women, a definition undoubtedly writted by a man.

**Post Office Censorship.** A ruling by the Postmaster General in 1943 said in revoking Esquire's second-class mail privilege: "A publication to enjoy these unique mail privileges and special preferences is bound to do more than refrain from disseminating material which is obscene or bordering on the obscene. It is under a positive duty to contribute to the public good and the public welfare." The U.S. Supreme Court replied: "But the power to determine whether a periodical (which is mailable) contains information of a public character, literature or art does not include the further power to determine whether the contents meet some standard of the public good or welfare." *Hannegan v. Esquire.* In short, the post office is not supposed to make decisions on the quality of content of a periodical.

**Precedent.** A previous court decision used to decide a present case of similar facts. Courts are hierarchical in structure. Thus, the higher the court, the more the decision makes precedent. Decisions of state supreme courts are binding on all courts within that state but have no direct precedent value in other states; but state jurists will look at similar cases in other states and can be influenced by well reasoned decisions. Similarly, a U.S. Court of Appeals decision rules only those federal district courts within the appeals circuit, but again a strong decision can influence the decision on similar cases in other districts. On First Amendment matters, the U.S. Supreme Court is the final decision, binding on all courts in the United States, state or federal. Lower courts, however, sometimes have difficulty figuring out what the high court ruling is exactly or how it applies to new situations, in which case new appeals either modify or confirm the precedent. Each confirmation makes the precedent stronger.

**Preferred Position.** An approach to First Amendment questions which holds that legislation touching on such fundamental constitutional rights should be given a more thorough judicial review than ordinary legislation to which courts traditionally grant some presumption of constitutionality.

**Preponderance of Evidence.** The standard used in civil law suits to decide who wins. Proof beyond reasonable doubt is required for conviction in a criminal case. The preponderance standard was replaced in libel suits involving public officials and public figures by a more demanding standard of clear and convincing evidence that the alleged libeller had engaged in knowing falsehood or reckless disregard of the truth.

**Press.** The word "press" in freedom of the press means the function of journalism regardless of the media. It has always covered more than newspapers. "The press in its historic connotation comprehends every sort of publication which affords a vehicle of information and opinion." *Lovell v. Griffin.* Print media is more covered by the First Amendment than are movies, radio or television in that no pre-screening of print is constitutionally tolerable and no Fairness Doctrine applies to print. But the content of news or opinion via broadcasting has the same First Amendment standing as content in print media.

**Press Card.** A means of reporter identification, it is usually issued by a police department on the recommendation of the media or through some screening committee of print and broadcast journalists. A press card has no legal standing. It's a convenience to media to permit their representatives to go through police or fire lines or other places requiring some identification. Police departments can establish "reasonable classification" rules to determine who gets a press card. *Los Angeles Free Press v. City of Los Angeles.* However, in a Washington lawsuit over denial of press credentials, the Secret Service was ordered to set up standards in "as precise terms as possible" to govern the issuing of such credentials, to tell a reporter in writing why he is denied a pass, and to provide a procedure for appealing the denial. *Forcade v. Knight.*

**Prime Time Access Rule.** A 1969 Federal Communications Commission rule that local broadcast stations, network-owned or affiliated, in the top 50 markets devote one hour between 7 and 11 p.m. to non-network programs. In 1974, the rule was modified to the half hour between 7:30 and 8 p.m. with a number of exceptions, e.g. Sundays, network children's programs, overruns of sports events. The rule's purpose is to reduce network dominance by encouraging other program sources, preferable locally-originated programs. The rule was upheld as a proper exercise of FCC power. *Mt. Mansfield Television v. FCC.*

**Prime Time Censorship Rule.** Another name for the Family Viewing Policy, so-called by its critics.

**Printers' Ink Statute.** A model statute developed in 1911 by the trade magazine, Printers' Ink, dealing with deceptive advertising and subsequently adopted widely by state government. It holds the source of the advertisement responsible for a misdemeanor for "any assertion, representation or statement of fact which is untrue, deceptive or misleading."

**Prior Restraint.** When a court orders news or commentary not to be printed or broadcast, the order is called a prior restraint because it acts to prevent any dissemination of whatever is banned. To violate such an order is direct contempt of court. The U.S. Supreme Court holds that prior restraint can be constitutional if a heavy burden of proof is met that some irreparable damage will be done if the restraint is not allowed. But in controlling cases from 1931 to 1977, the court viewed prior restraint as presumptively unconstitutional and did not find sufficient reason to allow it. Media sees prior restraint as censorship pure and simple. The court, while not ruling it out under all circumstances, regards it as "the most serious and the least tolerable infringement on First Amendment rights." *Nebraska Press Association v. Stuart.*

**Privacy.** The right to be let alone, to avoid attention by media. That such a right exists is recognized in U.S. Supreme Court decisions, but case law has some distance to go before the fence lines are defined between media's right to report and a right of privacy. Public officials and public figures are seen as having less right to privacy than private individuals. News from court records or other public records does not invade privacy, but here and there courts have shown some sensitivity to the re-use of old records, particularly criminal records after the felon has been rehabilitated *(Briscoe v. Reader's Digest)*, to unnecessary use (in the eyes of the court) of a person's name *(Barber v. Time)*, and to intrusion by subterfuge to gather news *(Dietemann v. Time)*. Commercial use of another's name or picture without permission is actionable under privacy in most states. Privacy deals with damage to the personality through embarrassment, libel deals with damage to reputation. "...however it may be ultimately defined, there is a zone of privacy surrounding every individual, a zone within which the state may protect him from intrusion by the press, with all its attendant publicity." *Cox Broadcasting Co. v. Cohn.* See False Light.

**Privacy Act of 1974.** A federal law which limits the gathering and use by federal agencies of information relating to individuals, increases a person's right to see what information the government has on him and to correct errors therein, and provides criminal penalties for misuse of such information. The law also set up a seven-member Privacy Protection Study Commission to study such areas as private data banks, local government data banks, and the storage and use of information by banks, insurance companies and educational institutions. The act reflects a growing concern about invasion of privacy in the sense of the use of personal information by government and major private agencies.

**Privilege—Absolute.** On the premise that "officials of government should be free to exercise their duties unembarrassed by the fear of damage suits . . . which might appreciably inhibit the fearless, vigorous, and effective administration of policies of government," such officials are immune from libel or slander suits. *Barr v. Matteo.* This privilege is called absolute. It covers "judges of courts of superior or general authority . . . in the exercise of their judicial functions . . . (and) other officers of government whose duties are related to the judicial process." It covers executive officers to the "outer perimeter" of their duties, and it covers legislators speaking or writing within their responsibilities as law makers. How far down the levels of government the privilege goes is not certain, but "the higher the post, the broader the range of responsibilities and duties, and the wider the scope of discretion" the more certain the privilege becomes. The privilege attaches also to quasi-judicial proceedings, for example, hearings before a workman's compensation board or a public utility commission. It covers lawyers, jurors and other participants in court actions made within the proceedings, witnesses before legislative hearings, documents and reports from department heads, and elected officials. Town supervisors, policemen, school board members have been held to have conditional not absolute privilege, but cases are infrequent, hence the uncertainty about lower levels. Documents required to be published by statute or court order have absolute immunity as does a broadcast station for defamation by a political candidate whose broadcast comes under his right of reply within the Fairness Doctrine. The station is not permitted to edit his speech and therefore has been held immune.

**Privilege—Conditional.** Journalism has a conditional or qualified privilege to report any statements arising in arenas of absolute privilege, the condition being that the report be accurate and without malice. This conditional privilege means an immunity from libel suits. As one example of how it works, a number of persons were identified in 1969 before a subcommittee on organized crime of the U.S. Senate as members of the Mafia. News reports since have repeated the identifications without jeopardy of libel. Most of the news that damages someone's reputation comes from privileged sources—indictments, informations, legislative testimony, reports of formal investigations by government auditors, by attorneys general or by regulatory agencies.

**Procedural Due Process.** With some narrow exceptions such as people being endangered for lack of prompt government action, procedural due process requires some form of notice or hearing before a citizen is deprived of property or of a protected freedom like freedom of the press.

**Program Responsibility Doctrine.** Under Federal Communications Commission rules, the selection of programs is solely the responsibility of the licensee and can not be delegated by the licensee to any network or other person or group, nor can the licensee enter into any contractual arrangements which restrict the licensee in exercising his independent judgments. Under this doctrine, the hundreds of licensees are required to satisfy their own judgment as to suitable programming and are not to abdicate this responsibility to the networks, to program consultants or to civic groups.

# p

**Property Right in News.** Independent of copyright, there is an ownership right to news based on the investment and labor that goes into its gathering and distribution. A news event itself is in the public domain. Its presentation in a particular form of words and pictures is copyrightable. But news is also a kind of merchandise legitimately for sale by a business enterprise. Taking news acquired by another's "expenditure of labor, skill, and money" and reselling it is actionable under unfair competition because such action is "an unauthorized interference" with a legitimate business and gives an unfair competitive advantage to the news pirate who "is not burdened with any part of the expense of gathering the news." *International News Service v. Associated Press.*

**Pseudonymous Work (Copyright).** A work on the copies or phonorecords of which the author is identified under a fictitious name.

**Publication (Copyright).** The distribution of copies or phonorecords of a work to the public by sale or other transfer of ownership, or by rental, lease, or lending, or the offering to distribute copies or phonorecords to a group of persons for purposes of further distribution, public performance or public display.

**Publication (Libel).** Communication of a defamation to a third party (someone other than the person originating the defamation and the person defamed). Publication requires an intention to so communicate or that reasonable foresight would know that the defamation would be circulated to a third party.

**Public Domain.** When a copyright expires, the material goes into the public domain. It becomes public property and anyone can use it without permission.

**Public Figure.** A private person and a public figure have different relationships in libel. The latitude for journalism is larger in the latter category. The U.S. Supreme Court describes a public figure this way: "In some instances an individual may achieve such pervasive fame or notoriety that he becomes a public figure for all purposes and in all contexts. More commonly, an individual voluntarily injects himself or is drawn into a particular public controversy and thereby becomes a public figure for a limited range of issues. In either case such persons assume special prominence in the resolution of public questions." *Gertz v. Welch.*

# p

**Public Interest, Convenience and Necessity.** The controlling words in the congressional grant of authority to the Federal Communications Commission. Licensed media must operate within FCC rules devised to achieve the standards implied in this charter phrase. "The 'public interest' to be served under the Communications Act is thus the interest of the listening public..." and does not confine the FCC to merely "finding that there are no technological objections to the granting of a license," but the phrase does not empower the FCC "to choose among applicants on the basis of their political, economic, or social views, or upon any other capricious basis." *National Broadcasting Co. v. United States.* The phrase is the legal standard for operating licensed facilities under federal law as determined by the FCC.

**Public Law of Libel.** The aggregate of those cases which put public officials and public figures in a different category than private citizens in relation to libel. The cases, beginning with *New York Times v. Sullivan,* make it more difficult for public persons to sue successfully. The underlying theory is that democracy is better served by free and frank discussion of public issues and persons thereto connected and that fear of libel could inhibit robust discussion. Actual malice is the governing rule in the public law of libel. Some texts call it the constitutional privilege.

**Public Meetings.** In concept, meetings of elected or appointed public officials to do public business are public meetings, but the exceptions are many. Legislative bodies meet publicly for final actions but closed doors for caucuses or committee sessions are common. The judiciary is open in its several steps (preliminary hearings, arraignments, trials) but occasionally judges close some parts of the process, or try to, on the argument usually of some jeopardy to the defendant. Executive agencies are open but retreat to closed executive sessions to discuss sensitive matters (e.g. labor contracts, disciplining of an employee, consultation with the agency's attorney on a lawsuit). In the 1970's several states enacted sunshine laws which severely restrict the occasions on which executive agencies or local governments and their agencies can close a meeting. Democratic theory, of course, argues that a government by the people should be open to the people, and one of the historically important functions of media has been to insist on a maximum of open meetings. See Public Records.

**Public Notice Advertising.** See Legal Advertising.

**Public Official.** For purposes of the New York Times rule in libel, the term applies "at the very least to those among the hierarchy of government employees who have, or appear to the public to have, substantial responsibility for or control over the conduct of governmental affairs." *Rosenblatt v. Baer.* And, "The employee's position must be one which would invite public scrutiny and discussion of the person holding it, entirely apart from the scrutiny and discussion occasioned by the particular controversy." Subsequent decisions have included a city commissioner, police chief, deputy sheriff, an elected court clerk and county attorney. How far the term covers down the ranks of government is not certain.

**Public Performance or Display (Copyright).** This means 1. to perform or display it at a place open to the public or at any place where a substantial number of persons outside of a normal circle of a family and its social acquaintances is gathered; or 2. to transmit or otherwise communicate a performance or display of the work to a place specified in 1 or to the public, by means of any device or process, whether the members of the public capable of receiving the performance or display receive it at the same place or in separate places and at the same time or at different times.

**Public Record.** Any record which law requires a public officer or public body to keep as a memorial of the actions of the official or the agency is a public record, unless it is exempted by a specific statute or decree having the force of law. The right to inspect a public record is well established in English common law but modified by requiring the seeker to show some proper interest in the record sought. The modern trend is seen in the Federal Freedom of Information Act and similar laws in state governments—no reason need be given why the record is sought, and the burden for showing cause for denial is on the agency. The concept of democratic self-government also requires that more than less records be open, else the people are unable to find out how their government through agents is performing. Journalism pushes for the maximum of open records, but generally accepts also that public policy is sometimes better served by closed records (e.g. persons being treated for venereal disease where state public health authority has to be notified; underworld informers to the police; diplomatic correspondence; military records valuable to an enemy power). The case for public records is stated in *Cox Broadcasting Co. v. Cohn:* "Public records by their very nature are of interest to those concerned with the administration of government, and a public benefit is performed by the reporting of the true contents of the records by the media. The freedom of the press to publish that information appears to us to be of critical importance to our type of government in which the citizenry is the final judge of the proper conduct of public business."

**Public Trial.** The Sixth Amendment of the U.S. Constitution guarantees that "the accused shall enjoy the right to a speedy and public trial." State constitutions have identical or similar language. The confrontation issue between media and the judiciary lies in whether the "public trial" is a right of a defendant to be waived if he or she sees fit or the public's right and to be denied, if at all, only under extraordinary circumstances. The issue extends to pre-trial hearings as well as to the trial itself. Media agrees with the reasoning that a pre-trial hearing is often the critical stage in a criminal prosecution because unwarranted police practices or dubious plea bargaining may be brought to light therein, and that closing to the public any part of the trial process requires at least that such closure be "strictly and inescapably necessary to protect the interests asserted by the defendant." *United States v. Cianfrani.* Much dicta exist to the effect that what takes place in an open courtroom is the public's business but these dicta do not quite say that the courtroom must always be open. The weight of American history, however, stands against close-door trials. Justice Hugo L. Black expressed this view in 1948. "We have been unable to find a single instance of a criminal trial conducted *in camera* in any federal, state or municipal court during the history of this country," and he likened any such trial to the "practice of the Spanish Inquisition, to the excesses of the English Court of Star Chamber." *In re Oliver.* An increasing frequency of closings in the late 1970's appears an ominous development and one that eventually will require clarification by the U.S. Supreme Court.

**Public Utility.** An enterprise supplying the public with a necessary product or service and which must supply the service to all citizens who seek it (with exceptions such as allowable cutting off telephone service for non-payment of the bill). Some plaintiffs have claimed that newspapers without direct competition in a community and therefore dominating the market are a kind of public utility. Such newspapers should then be required to accept advertising from anyone offering it (if the advertisement itself contains no illegal matter). Courts have consistently ruled, however, that a newspaper ". . . is a business essentially private in its nature—as private as that of the baker, grocer, or milkman, all of whom perform a service on which, to a greater or less extent, the communities depend, but bear no such relation to the public as to warrant its inclusion in the category of business charged with the public use . . . a newspaper is a strictly private enterprise . . . ." *Shuck v. Carroll Daily Herald.*

**Publici Juris.** Common property. Anything belonging to the people at large. A news event is publici juris and cannot be copyrighted, but the form and wording of the news presentation can be copyrighted. "But the news element—the information respecting current events contained in the literary production—is not the creation of the writer, but is a report of matters that ordinarily are publici juris; it is the 'history of the day'." *International News Service v. Associated Press.*

**Puffery.** Exaggerated claims about a product or a service. Legally acceptable until such claims cross an invisible line and become deceptive advertising. ". . . such words as 'easy,' 'perfect,' 'amazing,' 'prime,' 'wonderful,' and 'excellent,' are regarded in law as mere puffing or dealer's talk ...." *Carlay v. FTC.* Under Federal Trade Commission actions against deceptive advertising, the latitude allowed for puffery has been considerably narrowed.

**Punitive Damages.** See Libel—Damages.

# r

**Radio Act of 1912, 1927.** The first version was essentially a point-to-point maritime communications statute which required federal licenses to operate radio transmitters but allowed the Secretary of Commerce and Labor, charged with administering the law, "no discretion whatever" to refuse a license to anyone "coming within the classification designated in the act." *Hoover v. Intercity Radio.* A later decision, *United States V. Zenith Radio Corp.*, denied him authority to regulate operating conditions (power, hours of service etc.) with the result that near chaos threatened. The 1927 Act established a Federal Radio Commission and gave it specific regulatory powers over radio licenses, frequencies and operating conditions. The present controlling legislation, the Communications Act of 1934, is substantially similar to the Radio Act of 1927. The guiding phrase "public convenience, interest or necessity" was carried over from the 1927 Act as was the denial to government of any power to directly censor program content. Fundamental to the 1927 Act and to the powers of the present commission is the concept that scarcity of channels requires government supervision. "Before 1927, the allocation of frequencies was left entirely to the private sector, and the result was chaos. It quickly became apparent that broadcast frequencies constituted a scarce resource . . ." needing government control or ". . . the medium would be of little use because of the cacophony of competing voices, none of which could be clearly and predictably heard." *Red Lion Broadcasting v. FCC.*

**Raised Eyebrow Regulation.** A phrase coined to describe the indirect force of a letter from the Federal Communications Commission to a licensee questioning some program practice. The letter is not a formal order of the FCC but merely "suggests" that the station review the practice since the FCC has had some complaint about it.

**Reardon Report.** Recommendations adopted by the American Bar Association in 1968 titled "Standards Relating to Fair Trial and Free Press." The report covers categories of information which defense and prosecuting attorneys in the ABA's view should and should not release to the press. The fact and circumstances of arrest and essential biographical information are proper but confessions, prior criminal records, performance of tests (e.g. lie detector) or refusal to take one, possibility of plea bargaining, conclusionary statements about guilt, or matters not on court record are banned in the Reardon recommendations. If the alleged criminal is at large, the prosecution may release any information "necessary to aid in his apprehension or to warn the public of any danger he may present." The report gets its name from Paul C. Reardon, Justice, Massachusetts Supreme Court, who headed the ABA committee appointed to study press-trial conflicts. The recommendations are not legally binding. Court orders are sometimes issued banning trial participants from giving such information to reporters, but that's a separate matter. Revision of the Reardon Report was under study by the ABA in 1978.

**Reasonable Access Rule.** Broadcast stations must allow reasonable access to paid or free time for candidates for federal office, specifically; and by interpretation of this policy for unspecified candidates for state and local offices, but the station need not include the whole multitude of non-federal candidates common in general election years. The rule applies to legally-qualified candidates, i.e. candidates who have announced or those legally nominated.

**Reasonable Tendency Doctrine.** The doctrine that words are punishable which have a reasonable tendency to frustrate justice, to cause a breach of the peace, or to interfere with government generally. Constructive contempt, criminal libel and sedition were judged by this standard. The doctrine did not require proof that any damaging effect actually took place. "Again it is said there is no proof that the mind of the judge was influenced or his purpose to do his duty obstructed or restrained by the publications and therefore there was no proof tending to show the wrong complained of. But here again not the influence upon the mind of the particular judge is the criterion but the reasonable tendency of the acts done to influence or bring about the baleful result is the test." *Toledo Newspaper Co. v. United States.* Reasonable tendency has been replaced by the clear and present danger doctrine which requires for punishment an immediate and very serious threat to government. The rule of reasonable tendency was much more restrictive on media than the doctrine which replaced it.

**Redeeming Social Importance.** A phrase used in a 1957 landmark obscenity case, *Roth v. United States,* to describe why obscenity is not included in the First Amendment. The opinion of the court said: "All ideas having even the slightest redeeming social importance—

unorthodox ideas, controversial ideas, even ideas hateful to the prevailing climate of opinion—have the full protection of the guarantees, unless excludable because they encroach upon the limited area of more important interests. But implicit in the history of the First Amendment is the rejection of obscenity as utterly without redeeming social importance."

**Release Date.** The time given on the face of a publicity handout which says when it is available for media use. It's an arrangement of convenience for news sources and media both. Breaking a release date by premature use is not considered a legal problem except for the possibility that the release is protected by common law copyright (pre-1978) or is formally copyrighted under the new law.

**Release Form.** A document which permits the use of material, particularly photographs, in whatever way is specified in the release. Advertising agencies commonly use release forms in dealing with models to prevent any suits for invasion of privacy based upon commercial use of the person's picture. A release form, of course, should neither be drawn or signed without advice of an attorney.

**Remittitur.** "The jury returned a verdict for $60,000 in general damages and for $3,000,000 in punitive damages. The trial court reduced the total to $460,000 by remittitur." *Curtis Publishing Co. v. Butts*. The term describes the power of a judge to reduce an excessive verdict. Its opposite is additur.

**Reported Case.** The opinion of a court as reported in any of several reporting services; that is, the opinions that end up in bound volumes on library shelves. Not all cases are reported. Lower state court decisions rarely are and some states select which appellate court decisions are to be published, eliminating those which are routine in order to keep the volume of reported cases to manageable proportions. All U.S. Court of Appeals and U.S. Supreme Court decisions are reported.

**Reporter Certification.** Any form of government licensing of a reporter is a violation of the First Amendment. There are, however, some certifications of reporters. Secret Service clearance is required to cover the president; the military accredits reporters covering a war; the standing committee of correspondents controls the accreditation of reporters covering Congress; the executive committee of the Periodical Correspondents Association determines who has access to the periodical press galleries of the House and Senate; many state legislatures have correspondents associations which determine who can use the limited facilities of press rooms; and press cards issued by police departments are a quasi-certification which usually allow a reporter access through police and fire lines. These forms of accreditation or certification are not considered to be licensing.

**Res Judicata.** A question judicially acted upon, a decided case. It means that no new lawsuit can be brought on the same facts by the same parties.

**Respondeat Superior.** The words mean "let the master answer." It expresses the doctrine that the publisher may possibly be responsible for libel or invasion of privacy by the reporter. In an invasion of privacy suit against a Cleveland, Ohio newspaper, the U.S. Supreme Court said: "However, there was sufficient evidence for the jury to find that Eszterhas' writing of the feature was within the scope of his employment at The Plain Dealer and that Forest City Publishing Company was therefore liable under traditional doctrines of *respondeat superior.*" *Cantrell v. Forest City Publishing.*

**Responsibility.** "A responsible press is an undoubtedly desirable goal, but press responsibility is not mandated by the Constitution and like many other virtues it cannot be legislated." *Miami Herald v. Tornillo.* Obviously, however, irresponsibility can be punished after the fact by damages for libel as one example.

**Restatement of Torts.** Judges in media law cases sometimes use this as a source for clarification of obscure points or for supporting arguments. It is a publication of the American Law Institute which updates tort law on the basis of judicial decisions and on what it believes to be sound policy.

**Retraction.** The correction of error by printing or broadcasting the correction. Many states have retraction statutes related to libel. If the newspaper retracts, the usual requirement is that the retraction be given the same prominence as the alleged libel. The retraction operates to mitigate damages if the libel suit is successful. Media should correct its mistakes for reasons of ethical responsibility but correcting a possible libel should be done only with the advice of counsel.

# r

**Right of Publicity.** The concept that celebrities have a property right in their identity and should have control over the use of their names or pictures. Unauthorized commercial use of a person's identity is generally actionable under the broad umbrella of privacy. The thrust of privacy, however, is a right to be let alone, whereas celebrities often do not so much want to be let alone as to be sure they control the dollar value of their identities. A right of publicity has been upheld in the U.S. Supreme Court. Hugo Zacchini, the "human cannonball" sued on the grounds that a TV report of his 15-second performance was an unlawful appropriation of his exclusive rights to his identity. The Ohio Supreme Court ruled against him, reasoning: "The proper standard must necessarily be whether the matters reported were of public interest, and if so, the press will be liable for appropriation of a performer's right of publicity only if its actual intent was not to report the performance, but rather to appropriate the performance for some other private use, or if the actual intent was to injure the performer." *Zacchini v. Scripps-Howard.* The U.S. Supreme Court disagreed: "We are quite sure that the First and Fourteenth Amendments do not immunize the media when they broadcast a performer's entire act." The court reasoned in part from a parallel to copyright, that copyright is meant to encourage original works by giving the copyright owner certain controls over the use of the creative product.

**Right of Reply.** Through the Fairness Doctrine and through regulations governing equal time, political attacks and political editorials, some right of reply exists in licensed media. No right of reply to an attack exists in print media. "A newspaper is more than a passive receptacle or conduit for news, comment, and advertising. The choice of material to go into a newspaper, and the decisions made as to limitations on the size of the paper, and content, and treatment of public issues and public officials—whether fair or unfair—constitutes exercise of editorial control and judgment. It has yet to be demonstrated how governmental regulation of this crucial process can be exercised consistent with First Amendment guarantees of a free press as they have evolved to this time." *Miami Herald v. Tornillo.*

**Right to Know.** Journalism's claim to rights under the First Amendment is sometimes phrased as the "right to know," meaning the people's right to know what government is doing. The phrase appears in many law cases, usually affirmatively, but no precise boundaries of a "right to know" have been legally defined. There is a common law right to examine public records, which by inference is a right to know. In political theory, a democracy needs an informed citizenry and therefore there is a right to know what public officials are doing else citizens could not make informed judgments on the quality of government.

**Right to Receive Information.** Justice William J. Brennan Jr., concurring that a federal law restricting a citizen's right to receive communist mail from abroad, opined that the "right to receive publications" is one of the "fundamental personal rights" of a citizen. "The dissemination of ideas can accomplish nothing if otherwise willing addressees are not free to receive and consider them. It would be a barren marketplace of ideas that had only sellers and no buyers." *Lamont v. Postmaster General.* This "right to receive" does not include obscene materials through the mails or a right to transport them.

**Right to Refuse Advertising.** The First Amendment prohibits government compelling any media to accept any advertisement. A modification of sorts of this doctrine occurs if one medium refuses advertising for the purpose of damaging competitive media in a way that brings the question under the Sherman Antitrust Act. As a condition to advertising in his newspaper, a publisher cannot without antitrust jeopardy force an advertiser to boycott competitive media. *Lorain Journal v. United States.*

**Rolled-up Plea.** Fact and opinion not always being easily distinguishable, a "rolled-up" plea is used in some jurisdictions in defending against a libel suit. The defendant claims that anything judged to be opinion is fair comment and anything judged to be fact is true.

# S

**Scarcity Doctrine.** Underlying the idea that licensing of broadcast media is acceptable under the First Amendment while licensing of print media is not is the scarce channels argument. Broadcast "space" is limited. The doctrine has been upheld in a number of cases, the line of reasoning being succinctly expressed in 1943 in *National Broadcasting Co. v. United States:* "...the radio spectrum simply is not large enough to accommodate everybody. There is a fixed natural limitation upon the number of stations that can operate without interfering with one another."

**Scienter.** In *Roth v. United States,* an obscenity case, the word appears this way in U.S. Supreme Court Justice Earl Warren's concurring decision. "The personal element in these cases is seen most strongly in the requirement of scienter. Under the California law, the prohibited activity must be done 'wilfully and lewdly.' The federal statute limits the crime to acts done 'knowingly'." The word means awareness, foreknowledge, or that a person reasonably should know that wrongdoing is involved in a particular action.

**Sculptural Word (Copyright).** See Pictorial Work.

**Search Warrant.** An order issued by a judge on a police showing that probably cause exists that a search will yield evidence relative to a crime. Using a search warrant to get material from media is a heavier weapon than using a *subpoena duces tecum.* The subpoena route gives the newspaper or broadcast station a chance for a court hearing on a motion to quash the order, whereas a search warrant is made effective by police at the door and provides no time to pre-contest its validity. Lower federal courts held that a warrant search of the Stanford Daily News violated the First Amendment rights of the newspaper. *Stanford Daily v. Zurcher.* Palo Alto police had used the warrant route in 1971 to rummage for notes, photographs or any information which might identify persons (not connected with the newspaper) who assaulted police during a demonstration at Stanford University Hospital. On May 31, 1978, the U.S. Supreme Court overturned the lower federal courts holdings, holding that ". . . the preconditions for a warrant—probable cause, specificity with respect to the place to be searched and the things to be seized, and overall reasonableness . . . ." were sufficient protection against First Amendment rights "assertedly threatened by warrants for searching newspaper offices." (The New York Times, 6/1/78, page 42). Justice Potter Stewart in dissent saw a grave threat to press freedom, arguing that warrant searches jeopardized the protection of source confidentiality "necessary to insure that the press can fulfill its constitutionally designated function of informing the public. . . ." He distinguished between the police "rummaging through the files, cabinets, desks and wastebaskets of a newsroom" and police searches of "the office of a doctor or the office of a bank" because the Constitution does not explicitly protect medicine or banking from "abridgement by Government" but it does "explicitly protect the freedom of the press." Media voices see the decision as a serious chilling-effect setback for press freedom, opening the door to circumventing confidence statutes where they exist and to potential police harassment of newsrooms. The law enforcement view which prevailed is that a newsroom should be treated the same as any other place where evidence might be found to help solve a crime.

**Second Class Mail.** A preferential mail rate created to encourage the spreading of knowledge and used historically and today by newspapers and magazines. Eligibility for the rate requires publication at intervals not less than quarterly, printed matter, not more than 75 percent advertising over a year's issues, a list of paid subscribers, not more than 10 percent free circulation, sorting of zip codes, and the publication must carry news of general interest or be dedicated to literature, art or science. The second class rate is affected by many variables—weight, number of pieces, and a zone system based on distance.

**Secrecy Agreement.** "The question for decision is the enforceability of a secrecy agreement exacted by the government, in its capacity as employer, from an employee of the Central Intelligence Agency. Marchetti contends that his First Amendment rights foreclose any prior restraint upon him in carrying out his purpose to write and publish what he pleases about the agency and its operations." *United States v. Marchetti.* The U.S. Court of Appeals, Fourth Circuit, disagreed and found no First Amendment violation in the secrecy agreement which required Marchetti to submit "any writing, fictional or non-fictional" to the agency for editing before publication. Victor Marchetti was enjoined from publishing without clearance. His book when published had blank spaces indicating 168 deletions made by the

CIA. Similar agreements—legally enforceable—are sometimes required in private industry from persons handling formulas or other trade secrets.

**Section 303.** (This and sections following are those parts of the Communications Act of 1934 which are mentioned with some frequency in texts on media law.) Establishes the authority of the Federal Communications Commission in a number of specific areas, including assignment of frequencies, hours of broadcast, records required of licensees, engineering and transmission qualities, suspension of license, and "the nature of the service to be rendered by each class of licensed station and each station within any class." It contains the general grant of authority to the FCC to "make such rules and regulations" as are necessary to do its job.

**Section 307.** Requires allocation of licenses in a way that "shall make such distribution of licenses, frequencies, hours of operation, and of power among the several states and communities as to provide a fair, efficient, and equitable distribution" of service, and sets the terms of licenses and authority over renewals.

**Section 315.** The section of the Communications Act of 1934 which governs equal opportunity for candidates to use broadcasting time, commonly called the equal time provision. As amended in 1959, the section also caries language which expresses the sense of the Fairness Doctrine, and that language is used to support rules of the Federal Communications Commission governing personal attack and political editorializing. The U.S. Supreme Court holds that FCC regulations under Section 315 do not violate First Amendment rights of licensees. "Licenses to broadcast do not confer ownership of designated frequencies but only the temporary privilege of using them." And "there is nothing in the First Amendment which prevents the government from requiring a licensee to share his frequency with others . . . ." And "although broadcasting is clearly a medium affected by a First Amendment interest, differences in the characteristics of new media justify differences in the First Amendment standards applied to them." *Red Lion Broadcasting v. FCC.*

**Section 317.** Requires that all paid matter broadcast be identified as to the source paying, including indirect payments or promises but excluding services or property nominally furnished by the broadcaster. This requirement can be waived by the Federal Communication Commission when it determines that "the public interest, convenience or necessity does not require the broadcasting of such announcement.''

**Section 326.** The section of the Communications Act of 1934 which denies the Federal Communications Commission any ''power of censorship'' over licensed media by stating that no FCC regulation ''shall interfere with the right of free speech by means of radio or television communication.'' The idea ought not to be taken literally since the FCC does impose sanctions on profanity, rigged contests, and gambling information; pressures stations against playing drug-oriented music; and regulates network relations with affiliate stations. Further, the FCC takes into account in license renewals the station's general performance in the public interest, thereby influencing by its criteria of acceptable performance the kind of programming the licensee provides.

**Section 396.** Declares ''that it is in the public interest to encourage the growth and development of noncommercial radio and television broadcasting.'' And sets up the Corporation for Public Broadcasting with six-year terms for its 15 members who are appointed by the president with the advice and consent of the Senate, and itemizes PBC objectives as a nonprofit and nonpolitical corporation.

**Section 399.** ''No noncommercial educational broadcasting station may engage in editorializing or may support or oppose any candidate for political office.'' The prohibition originates in the Public Broadcasting Act of 1967 and contrasts with the right of commercial broadcasters to editorialize and support political candidates.

**Section 508.** Requires that any radio station employee accepting outside money or gifts in exchange for broadcasting, say, a particular record, must disclose the ''payola'' received or face a possible fine of up to $10,000 or a sentence of not more than one year.

**Self Censorship.** If words or pictures printed or broadcast did not have the protection of the First Amendment, writers and speakers would become overly cautious to avoid punishment for expressing their thoughts. This is the concept of self censorship. The threat itself of punishment after the fact inhibits freedom. If First Amendment freedoms are enlarged by court decisions, less self censorship takes place; if narrowed, more. Many decisions point to self censorship as a reason for taking great care in deciding First Amendment cases. ''A rule compelling the critic of official conduct to guarantee the truth of all his factual assertions—and to do so on pain of libel judgments virtually unlimited in amount—leads to . . . 'self censorship'." *New York Times v. Sullivan.*

**Sequester.** To set aside or isolate. A jury is sequestered when it is "locked up" overnight in a hotel under court supervision and denied access to any information other than the testimony in the trial. Sequestration is recommended by the U.S. Supreme Court when necessary to assure that jurors are not influenced by any trial publicity. Since some trials run on for weeks, sequestration can be a hardship on a juror. The Florida Supreme Court, however, expressed the view that jury hardship should be a secondary consideration. "The inconvenience suffered by jurors who are sequestered to prevent exposure to excluded evidence which may be published in the press is a small price to pay for the public's right to timely knowledge of trial proceedings guaranteed by freedom of the press." *Florida ex rel. Miami Herald v. McIntosh.*

**Service Mark.** See Trademark.

**Shield Laws.** State laws governing the right of a journalist to refuse to testify before a grand jury, in a trial or before a legislative committee about sources of information or information not used (notes and outtakes). Twenty-five states have such laws. There is no federal shield law. Precisely who is shielded and under what circumstances varies with the wording of the particular statute and its judicial interpretation. In California, for example, faced with a shield law which barred compulsory disclosure of sources or of information not used, the court ruled that its inherent power to insure the orderly administration of justice outweighed the statute. As a result, four editorial employees of the Fresno Bee went to jail for refusing to reveal who had leaked sealed grand jury testimony. *Rosato v. Superior Court of Fresno County.* Media voices are ambivalent about shield laws. Some argue that some protection, though imperfect, is better than none. Others argue that it is dangerous to have a legislature involved in defining who is a journalist and that the issue should be fought on First Amendment grounds as it arises. The U.S. Supreme Court, however, has said clearly that there is no First Amendment right to refuse to testify. See Newsman's (Woman's) Privilege.

**Shopper.** A free-distribution publication devoted wholly to advertising or designed to circulate advertising primarily rather than news.

**Shouting Fire.** Justice Oliver W. Holmes, describing his limit on freedom of expression, wrote: "The most stringent protection of free speech would not protect a man in falsely shouting fire in a crowded theatre and causing a panic." *Schenck v. United States.* The sentence is often misquoted by shortening it to: free speech doesn't protect someone shouting fire in a crowded theatre. Carefully read, the short version says something different than Holmes's original.

**Single Publication Rule.** A judicially evolved doctrine holding that liability for libel extends only to the single edition and not to every separate newspaper within the edition. Thus, a newspaper with 500,000 circulation cannot be sued 500,000 times for a single libel. This does not cover repetition of the same libel in different newspapers. If a dozen separate newspapers run the libel, the person defamed has the possibility of filing a dozen separate lawsuits. Twenty-three or more states have judicial precedent for the single publication rule and seven states have enacted the Uniform Single Publication Act.

**Siphoning.** This is said to occur "when an event or program currently shown on conventional free television is purchased by a cable operator for showing on a subscription cable channel." *Home Box Office v. FCC.* The possibility of siphoning creates a fear that the much smaller number of cable subscribers might by paying a fee per viewing hour preempt certain programs, first-run movies for example, from free television. Whether siphoning is in fact a real danger to standard TV is an unsettled argument.

**Sketching.** Is sketching of trial participants and publication of the sketches forbidden? A 1974 case which gives some guidance is *United States v. Columbia Broadcasting System.* In a pre-trial hearing of the "Gainesville Eight," accused of conspiracy to disrupt the 1972 Republican National Convention, the judge announced that "no sketches in the courtroom would be permitted to be made for publication." A CBS artist attended the hearing and made sketches later from memory. Learning of this, the judge expanded the order to include sketches from memory made outside the courtroom. CBS ran the sketches and was held in contempt of court. The U.S. Court of Appeals, Fifth Circuit, ruled the ban "too broadly drawn to withstand constitutional scrutiny." The ban was "too remotely related" to any jeopardy to any later fair trial for the defendants. Distinguishing sketching from the arguments in *Estes v. Texas* that television has an adverse effect on trial participants, the appeals court said: "To our knowledge, no state or federal court has prohibited the publication of sketches. Of the 80 federal district courts which have written rules, only three have provided . . . that in certain widely publicized cases the court may direct 'that . . . no photograph be taken or sketch made of any juror within the environs of the court'." The court said it was unwilling "to condone a sweeping prohibition of in-court sketching where there has been no showing whatsoever that sketching is in any way obtrusive or disruptive."

**Slander.** Oral defamation. Slander is considered less damaging than libel because its range is limited to those who heard it and it lacks the permancy of defamation in print. Decisions are uneven as to whether defamation by broadcasting is slander or libel but the trend seems to be toward libel.

**Slander per se.** Unlike libel per se (defamation on the face of it, obvious libel) slander per se has specific criteria. The defamation must fit one of these accusations: a criminal offense involving moral turpitude; a loathsome disease; unchastity in a female; unfitness for one's profession, trade, business, or calling. The understanding of the hearers of the defamation is controlling. Moral turpitude connotes a moral fault in a serious matter likely to cause some social disgrace rather than, say, failure to pay a parking ticket. Loathsome disease is veneral disease or leprosy.

**Slogans.** Not subject to copyright but they can be registered as trademarks or service marks. For registration the words have to be more than a mere statement of fact or discription of a product.

**Social Value Theory.** The theory that the First Amendment does not protect expression which has no "social value as a step to truth." The U.S. Supreme Court rules out "certain well-defined and narrowly limited classes of speech" (e.g. obscenity, fighting words, libel) because "such utterances are of no essential part of any exposition of ideas, and are of such slight social value as a step to truth that any benefit that may be derived from them is clearly outweighed by the social interest in order and morality...." *Chaplinsky v. New Hampshire.* See Redeeming Social Importance.

**Sound Recordings (Copyright).** Works that result from the fixation of a series of musical, spoken, or other sounds, but not including the sounds accompanying a motion picture or other audiovisual work, regardless of the nature of the material objects, such as disks, tapes, or other phonorecords, in which they are embodied.

**Stamps.** Black and white, but not colored, illustrations of U.S. postage stamps are legal in articles, books, journals, newspapers, or albums for philatelic, educational, historical or newsworthy purposes. Colored illustrations are permitted of cancelled foreign stamps. The same illustrations are permitted in philatelic advertising by legitimate dealers. Motion picture films or slides, in black and white or color, for use in telecasting are permissible. The U.S. Treasury Department requires that any negatives, plates or glossy prints be destroyed after their final use for the purpose for which they were made.

**Stamp Tax.** In 1712, the British Parliament put a tax on newspapers by requiring a stamp sold by the government to be placed on each copy. Opponents called the stamps "taxes on knowledge." The stamps were "one of the factors that aroused the American colonists to protest against taxation for the purposes of the home government; and that the revolution really began when, in 1765, that government sent stamps for newspaper duties to the American colonies." *Grosjean v. American Press.*

**Standard Broadcast Station.** "A broadcasting station licensed for transmission of radiotelephone emissions primarily intended to be received by the general public and operated on a channel in the band 535—1605 kilocycles per second." *Title 37 C.F.R. Section 73.1*

**Standing.** A person or a group has "standing" in a lawsuit if some reasonably close connection exists between the issue of the suit and adverse or favorable effects of its outcome. Intervention in renewals of broadcast licenses were once limited to parties who could show some economic injury or electrical interference with their normal lives. In 1966, in *Office of Communication of United Church of Christ v. FCC,* members of that church in Jackson, Miss. were granted "standing" to intervene on the reasoning that licensees are required to operate in the "public interest" and therefore intervention by a part of the audience with a particular complaint about discrimination in programming is justified. The court said that " 'hosts' of protesters" need not be granted standing but that groups that "usually concern themselves with a wide range of community problems and tend to be representatives of broad rather than narrow interests" would be the kind of "responsible and representative groups" that are "eligible to intervene." The decision opened the door to citizen groups to be heard in license renewals.

**Stare Decisis.** Let the precedent stand. The doctrine that courts should lean toward following precedent when deciding cases with similar facts. The argument for the doctrine is that it gives stability to law and makes it easier for a citizen to know where he stands. The argument against it is that it tends to hold the dead hand of the past on decisions made in a different social and economic environment.

**State Action.** Since the First Amendment protects speech and press from abridgement by government only, and does not apply directly to restrictions or censorship by private individuals, the concept of state action, i.e. some governmental connection, direct or indirect, is required to justify a court's involvement in the issue. The term cannot be precisely defined. It's distinctive purpose is described in *Writers Guild v. FCC*. "The state action concept stands for the principle that individuals, in the absence of valid government regulation, are free to be ornery in their private lives; that in the absence of powers delegated to the federal government, state governments, within constitutional limits, have the primary responsibility to regulate private wrongdoing; and that to the extent that the federal government does have power to regulate private conduct, that power is legislative and not judicial. Thus the state action concept counsels that government invasions of constitutional liberties are to be prevented without unnecessarily imposing limitations on private autonomy." On the other hand, "non-governmental combinations," cannot use the First Amendment "as a refuge if they impose restraints upon that constitutionally guaranteed freedom." *Associated Press v. United States*.

**Statement of Ownership.** "Each owner of a publication having periodical publication mail privileges shall furnish to the Postal Service at least once a year . . . ." a statement of ownership, management and circulation. The statement requires the names of editor, managing editor, publisher and owners of more than one percent of corporate stocks or bonds and the press run broken down into paid and free circulation. Title 39 U.S.C.A. Section 4369.

**Stationers Company.** A printer's guild, established by Queen Elizabeth I in 17th century England, to regulate printing. Its members were among the first censors, and were required to control words written that criticized the Crown. In return for their services, the Queen

# S

granted company members economic protection, monopolies and other privileges. The company, and all such censorship, fell after the Glorious Revolution of 1689. Prior restraint officially died in England in 1695, when Parliament refused to renew the licensing and censorship laws.

**Statute of Limitations.** A law which puts a calendar limit on the right to take legal actions in particular cases, the calendar varying with the issue. Libel has a one-year statute of limitations in 28 states, two-year in 17 states, and three-year in four states and six-year in one state.

**Statutory Law.** Enactments by legislative bodies and approved by the executive or passed over his veto. "Statutory words are uniformly presumed, unless the contrary appears, to be used in their ordinary and usual sense, and with the meaning commonly attributed to them." *Caminetti v. United States.*

**Stipulation (FTC).** A written agreement, more formal and detailed than a letter of compliance, by which the advertiser agrees to stop practices which the Federal Trade Commission finds misleading. A stipulation does not eliminate possible further FTC action against the advertiser.

**Sua Sponte.** In *Sheppard v. Maxwell,* the 1965 decision of the U.S. Supreme Court relating to free press-fair trial issues, Justice Tom C. Clark, writing the opinion of the court, said: "sequestration of the jury was something the judge should have raised *sua sponte* with the jury." Sua sponte means voluntarily or of its own will.

**Sub Judice.** An issue before a court. "In the matter *sub judice,* even though the district court was legitimately concerned with preventing prejudicial publicity from poisoning the impartial atmosphere essential to a fair trial, we hold that the total ban on the publication of sketches is too remotely related to the danger sought to be avoided, and is, moreover, too broadly drawn to withstand constitutional scrutiny." *United States v. Columbia Broadcasting Systems.*

**Subpoena.** An order of a court to appear as a witness. A subpoena duces tecum is an order to bring specified records to court. Journalists subpoened to testify to their sources of news have no absolute First Amendment right to refuse, but in states with shield laws they have some rights to refuse depending on the wording of the statute and its interpretation by the court.

**Subscription Broadcast Stations.** Stations with the technical capability to broadcast TV programs intended to be received by the public only for a fee or charge.

**Substantial Service.** A phrase coined to define an attitude of the Federal Communications Commission toward an applicant for license renewal. The FCC will favor the present licensee if he has substantially serviced his community during the three-year license term, that is, he has presented a reasonable variety of programming and has not run afoul of the Fairness Doctrine, equal time or other FCC rules. The FCC prefers an acceptable record of performance to the promises of a challenger for a license. "Superior service" was urged as a better standard during a congressional review of FCC standards but did not prevail.

**Substantial Similarity.** Infringement in copyright is not limited to a literal, word-for-word use of copyrighted material without permission. Substantial similarity between the copy and the plagiarized work is sufficient. Thus paraphrasing of a copyrighted work does not automatically offset infringement. See Abstraction Test.

**Substantive Law.** The content of specific areas of law, e.g. contract law, estate law. It's distinct from adjective or procedural law which covers such things as rules of evidence, forms of pleadings. Adjective and substantive law work together to form the process of justice.

**Summary Judgment.** The action of a judge dismissing a case because no grounds exist to carry the case further. "The purpose of summary judgment is to avoid useless trials. When there are no genuine issues of material fact and a party is entitled to judgment as a matter of law, a trial court is justified in denying a trial on its merits." *Bandelin v. Pietsch.* Summary judgments are important to freedom of expression. "In the First Amendment area, summary procedures are even more essential. For the stake here, if harassment succeeds, is free debate. One of the purposes of the Times principle, in addition to protecting persons from being cast in damages in libel suits filed by public officials, is to prevent persons from being discouraged in the full and free exercise of their First Amendment rights with respect to the conduct of their government. The threat of being put to the defense of a lawsuit brought by a popular public official may be as chilling to the exercise of First Amendment freedoms as fear of the outcome of the lawsuit itself, especially to advocates of unpopular causes." *Washington Post v. Keogh.* Summary judgment, therefore, when applicable, works to prevent self-censorship through fear of the cost of defending against unwarranted libel suits. It serves to prevent "all but the strongest libel cases from proceeding to trial." *Martin Marietta Corp. v. Evening Star Newspaper.*

**Summary Proceeding.** Historically relevant to punishing constructive (indirect, out-of-court) contempt, under such a proceeding the judge who felt the contempt in the first place made the finding of guilt and imposed sentence without a jury and without the usual preliminary steps in a criminal action. The concept has been greatly modified by appellate court rulings or by statutes and its use against journalism is rarely, if at all, defensible today. See Wilmot's Doctrine.

**Sunshine Laws.** A phrase which describes laws requiring government meetings and public records to be open to the public and to the press. It refers more commonly to laws passed in the last several years in a number of states and at the federal level which have expanded access to meetings and records.

**Surrogate.** A person who acts in another's place as a substitute or deputy. Media in their journalism function sometimes are referred to as surrogates of the general public, that is, acting on its behalf under the assertion of the public's "right to know."

**Symbolic Speech.** The communication of an idea, usually a dissent, by actions (a sit-in, for example) or by a symbol (black arm bands). Generally, the U.S. Supreme Court has held that the First Amendment does not give "the same kind of freedom to those who would communicate ideas by conduct as the amendment affords to those who communicate ideas by 'pure speech'." *Cox v. Louisiana.* No certain line can be drawn as to when the symbol is more in the arena of action and thereby not as much protected or is more in the speech area and thereby within First Amendment protection. One guideline was expressed in upholding a conviction for burning a draft card. "When 'speech' and 'non-speech' elements are combined in the same course of conduct, a sufficiently important governmental interest in regulating the non-speech element can justify limitations on First Amendment freedoms." *United States v. O'Brien.* On the other hand, symbolic speech in the form of various treatments of the American flag, of hair styles, of arm bands, and of theatrical use of a military uniform has been upheld.

# S

**Syndicalism Laws.** From 1917 to 1920, criminal syndicalism statutes were adopted in 20 states and two territories. These laws were legislative reactions to fears that radical groups would overthrow the industrial or political order in the United States. Typically such laws made it a crime to "advocate or teach the duty, necessity or propriety" of violence "as a means of accomplishing industrial or political reform." *Brandenburg v. Ohio.* Assemblies for the purpose of such advocacy were illegal. In 1959, the U.S. Supreme Court in *Brandenburg* struck down the Ohio criminal syndicalism law, one typical of the genre, as violating the First and Fourteenth Amendments because it punished mere advocacy. In the 1920's these laws were used in several states to oppress radical groups.

**Tape Delay System.** Used by radio stations for programs involving phone calls from the audience, the system tapes the call and provides an automatic delay before the call goes on the air. Failure to use such a device was not in itself evidence of "reckless disregard of the truth" in a defamation case involving a public figure and station KFBC in Cheyene, Wyo. *Adams v. Frontier Broadcasting.* An earlier case in Louisiana holds that failure to use a delay does constitute reckless disregard. *Snowden v. Pearl River Broadcasting.* In *Adams,* the court held that open microphone talk shows were the modern equivalent of the town meeting and because they give citizens an opportunity to speak on public issues, they should not be inhibited by a delay requirement. The court also said that any relationship between reckless disregard and use of a delay was a question of fact (therefore requiring judgment in each case).

**Taxes on Knowledge.** "In 1792, in response to a message from Queen Anne, Parliament imposed a tax upon all newspapers and upon advertisements. That the main purpose of these taxes was to suppress the publication of comments and criticisms objectionable to the Crown does not admit of doubt. . . . These duties were quite commonly characterized as 'taxes on knowledge,' a phrase used for the purpose of describing the effect of the exactions and at the same time condemning them." *Grosjean v. American Press Co.* The *Grosjean* case declared unconstitutional a Louisiana tax on gross receipts from advertising in newspapers of more than 20,000 circulation, the purpose of which was to punish editors opposed to Huey Long.

**Term of Art.** " 'Actual malice' has become a term of art to provide a convenient shorthand for the New York Times standard of liability. It is quite different from the common law standard of 'malice' generally required under state tort law to support an award of punitive damages. Whereas the common law standard focuses on the defendant's attitude toward the plaintiff, 'actual malice' concentrates on the defendant's attitude toward the truth or falsity of the material published." *Carson v. Allied News Co.* Generally, term of art or word of art means that a word which has one meaning in literary

# t

usage may have different connotations when used by a particular trade or profession.

**Testimonials.** Endorsements of products or services as an advertising device are subject generally to the same controls as deceptive advertising. Affirmatively, some voluntary codes would limit testimonials to "competent witnesses" who reflect a "real choice" of the product (Advertising Code of American Business; The Creative Code of the American Society of Advertising Agencies). Ideally, a testimonial should be an honest and accurate opinion of a competent endorser, reflecting his or her present opinion and containing no misleading implications.

**Timely Disclosure.** A term important in financial public relations, this covers information which would influence investment decisions or the value of stocks or securities. It requires prompt release of such information to media so that all investors have the opportunity to be equally informed. Untrue statements or omission of significant facts are violations of Security and Exchange Commission regulations.

**Time of War.** Justice Oliver W. Holmes believed that the First Amendment had a different application in time of war. "When a nation is at war many things that might be said in time of peace are such a hindrance to its effort that their utterance will not be endured as long as men fight and that no court could regard them as protected by any constitutional right." *Schenck v. United States.* Justice Felix Frankfurter believed that the First Amendment "exacts obedience even during times of war" but he believed also that freedom of expression had to be balanced against other interests in each decision. "The demands of free speech in a democratic society as well as the interest in national security are better served by candid and informed weighing of the competing interests, within the confines of the judicial process . . . ." *Dennis v. United States.*

**Time, Place and Manner.** Reasonable "time, place and manner" regulations on speech and press are not violations of the First Amendment For example, a municipality can regulate the size, placement and housekeeping of newspaper vending machines or stalls. Such an ordinance, however, must not allow for any arbitrary judgment by municipal authorities which might infringe on freedom of the press. *Kash Enterprises v. Los Angeles.*

**Tort.** A branch of law dealing with damages or injuries not arising out of breach of contract. Libel suits are tort actions.

**Tortfeasor.** A feasor is one who does something. Libel is a tort. Originators of libels or those who publish them are tortfeasors.

**Trade Libel.** See Disparagement.

**Trademark.** "The term includes any word, name, symbol or device or any combination thereof adopted and used by a manufacturer or merchant to identify his goods and distinguish them from those manufactured or sold by others." Lanham Act, 1946. Its primary function is to identify the source of goods. A trademark is acquired by usage. Failure to police its usage can result in the trademark becoming a generic word. Media outlets are frequently asked by owners of valuable trademarks to capitalize the word. Thus, proper use by media is, for example, Coca-Cola or Coke, not coca-cola or coke. That the trademark is registered is shown by an R in a circle or by the statement, Registered in U.S. Patent Office (or abbreviated, Reg. U.S. pat. off.). Similar to trademarks are service marks (identifies the source in the sale or advertising of services), certification marks (e.g. marks indicating that the goods were made by union labor) and collective marks (cooperatives, associations or other collective groups).

**Trade Secrets.** Freedom of information statutes usually exempt trade secrets from records open to the public and to the press. It's a loose term whose boundaries are decided on a case-by-case judgment. Generally, it covers information, patterns, devices or formulas which give a business enterprise an advantage over competitors.

**Transfer of Ownership (Copyright).** An assignment, mortgage, exclusive license, or any other conveyance, alienation, or hypothecation of a copyright or of any of the exclusive rights comprised in a copyright, whether or not it is limited in time or place of effect, but not including a nonexclusive license.

**Transmit (Copyright).** To communicate a performance or display by any device or process whereby images or sounds are received beyond the place from which they are sent.

**Transmission Program (Copyright).** A body of material that, as an aggregate, has been produced for the sole purpose of transmission to the public in sequence and as a unit.

# t

**Trial by Newspaper.** A phrase used by critics of media to describe excessive publicity about a crime and trial to the possible jeopardy of the defendant's right to a trial by an unbiased jury. "The very word 'trial' connotes decisions on the evidence and arguments properly advance in open court. Legal trials are not like elections to be won through the use of the meeting hall, the radio, and the newspaper." U.S. Supreme Court Justice Hugo L. Black in *Bridges v. California*. "A trial is not a 'free trade in ideas,' nor is the best test of truth in a courtroom 'the power of the thought to get itself accepted in the competition of the market'...." Justice Felix Frankfurter, ibid. Media reporters, however, have on many occasions prevented or brought to light miscarriages of justice which otherwise would have gone unremedied had publicity not been focused on them. And ". . . pretrial publicity—even pervasive, adverse publicity—does not inevitably lead to an unfair trial." *Nebraska Press Association v. Stuart*. The Supreme Court in that case said the Nebraska court should use other powers than enjoining news reporting to assure a fair trial (e.g. the powers recommended in *Sheppard v. Maxwell*—continuance, change of venue, sequestration and voir dire).

**Truth.** A complete defense against a libel action in 39 states, the 11 other states adding that the publication must be made with good motives and justifiable ends. Once, the defense of truth required proving the defamation exactly true in all particulars; now the trend is to accept proof that the gist or the sting of the libel is true. The "truth" to be proven is not that someone was accurately quoted but that the content of the defamation itself is true. This point, however, may be modified by the recent doctrine of neutral reportage. Further, one court has held that a newspaper is not required to verify the truth in syndicated columns. "In many instances considerations of time and distance make verification impossible. Thus, the newspaper is confronted with the choice of publication without verification or suppression.... We should be hesitant to impose responsibilities upon newspapers which can be met only through costly procedures or through self-censorship designed to avoid risks of publishing controversial material." *Washington Post v. Keogh*. But the more common rule is that the newspaper is responsible at law for what it publishes.

**Two-level Theory.** The First Amendment protects some categories of expression but does not protect others, metaphorically a lower level of expression (e.g. obscenity, fighting words, defamatory lying). The U.S. Supreme Court separates the levels by fiat definitions. Essentially, the two-level theory is the same as definitional balancing. The standard used to define the lower level of unprotected expression is whether the expression has some redeeming value, some quality of social or political worth about it.

**Two-tiered Theory.** This view enunciated at length by U.S. Supreme Court Justice John M. Harlan in *Roth v. United States*, rejects that "just because the state may suppress a particular utterance, it is automatically permissible for the federal government to do the same." Harlan's argument, in part, is along these lines: "The Constitution differentiates between those areas of human conduct subject to the regulation of the states and those subject to the powers of the federal government. The substantive powers of the two governments, in many instances, are distinct. And in every case where we are called upon to balance the interest in free expression against other interests, it seems to me important that we should keep in the forefront the question of whether those other interests are state or federal. Since under our constitutional scheme the two are not necessarily equivalent, the balancing process must needs often produce different results."

**Tying.** In antitrust law, "...the forced purchase of a second distinct commodity with the desired purchase of a dominant 'tying' product, resulting in economic harm to competition in the 'tied' market." *Times-Picayune v. United States*. In that case, the U.S. Supreme Court held that requiring an advertiser to buy a combined insertion in morning and afternoon papers owned by the same publisher did not constitute tying within the meaning of the Sherman Antitrust Act. The court ruled that the newspapers were selling indistinguishable products, i.e. advertising space, and not forcibly selling an inferior by "tying" it to a dominant product.

# U

**Union Authorization Cards.** Such cards are considered sufficiently similar to medical and personnel records that they are exempt from disclosure under the Freedom of Information Act. "The cards contain what is, in effect, a thumb-nail sketch of an employee's job classification and status, in addition to the union authorization. Thus, we have no difficulty in deciding that the cards are 'similar files'." *Committee on Masonic Homes v. NLRB.* The U.S. Court of Appeals, Third Circuit, added: "To order disclosure here would effectively do away with union cards as they are now used" (because prospective members) "would be 'chilled' when asked to sign a union card if they knew the employer could see who signed." Further, union elections by secret ballot "would be directly undercut by forcing employees to acknowledge in public their support of the union, in order to be given the right to vote in secret for the union." The court found "a serious violation of privacy and no significant public interest in disclosure."

**Union Membership.** A publisher does not have a First Amendment right to discharge reporters on the sole basis of union membership. In 1937, the U.S. Supreme Court so held by ruling that the Associated Press was covered by the National Labor Relations Act. AP argued that ". . . it must have absolute and unrestricted freedom to employ and to discharge those who, like Watson, edit the news, that there must not be the slightest opportunity for any bias or prejudice personally entertained by an editorial employee to color or distort what he writes" and therefore "any regulation protective of union activity . . . is necessarily an invalid invasion of the freedom of the press." *Associated Press v. NLRB.* The court did not buy the premise that union membership automatically tainted the reporter. "The actual reason for his discharge, as shown by the unattacked finding of the board, was his guild activity and his agitation for collective bargaining." Morris Watson's victory removed the threat of such reprisals from the organizing efforts of the American Newspaper Guild, a union of editorial and business office employees.

**Useful Article (Copyright).** An article having an intrinsic utilitarian function that is not merely to portray the appearance of the article or to convey information. An article that is normally a part of a useful article is itself considered a useful article.

112

**USPS No. 2201.** If an individual wants his or her name taken off mailing lists advertising sexually-oriented materials, this U.S. Postal Service form is the vehicle. The postal service makes the 2201 form names available to mailers, and 30 days after a person's name is added to the list any mailer sending such material subjects himself to possible civil and criminal legal action.

**Variable Obscenity.** Erotic material which might not be punishable if distributed to adults can be punishable if distributed to minors. The "variable" is the variable of age and the justification is that "the state has an independent interest in the well-being of its youth." *Ginsberg v. New York*. On the other hand, material cannot be banned for adults on the grounds that it is unacceptable for minors because that would ". . . reduce the adult population . . . to reading only what is fit for children." *Butler v. Michigan*.

**Variable Venue.** Federal prosecutions for obscenity can be begun in the district of mailing or in any district through which the allegedly obscene material passes; thus, federal prosecutors can shop for locations where the chances of conviction are presumed to be more than less. Congress added this provision to federal obscenity law in 1958.

**Vel Non.** The judicial mind sometimes enjoys using archaic language. It seems to feel that obscurity enhances dignity. "It is important to stress that this analysis simply elaborates the test by which obscenity vel non of the material must be judged." *Ginzburg v. United States*. Vel non means "or not."

**Venue.** The county or district in which a case is to be tried. The U.S. Supreme Court recommends a change of venue as one way to lessen the effects of prejudicial publicity on prospective jurors. Pre-trial publicity is usually concentrated where the crime is committed or the criminal apprehended so persons in a distant part of the same state might not have read or seen as much about the case. Some crimes so dominate the news nationwide that a change of venue would seem not very helpful, the assassination of President John Kennedy, for example.

**Videotape.** As defined in the new copyright statute, it is "the reproduction of the images and sounds of a program or programs broadcast by a television broadcast station licensed by the Federal Communications Commission, regardless of the nature the material objects, such as tapes or films, in which the reproduction is embodied."

**Viewing Standard.** For purposes of cable system pickups, the Federal Communications Commission distinguishes between a local and a distant signal on a "viewing standard" formula. It's "local" if the signal is from an independent station and reaches two percent of the viewing hours in television homes and has a net weekly circulation of at least five percent. For network affiliates, the formula is three percent and 25 percent. "The two criteria reflect different concepts. Net weekly circulation reflects the extent to which signals are of any interest to television viewers but tends largely to reflect the availability or viewability of a signal as a technical matter. Audience share indicates the intensity of viewer interests." *36 FCC 2d 175.*

**Voir Dire.** The process of examining jurors to eliminate those whose predispositions make it unlikely that they could render an unbiased verdict. It is one of several powers a court has which can be used to minimize the effects of prejudicial pre-trial publicity. Voir means "to see." Dire means "to say." Its usefulness is indicated in this excerpt of an Iowa Supreme Court opinion: "A transcript of voir dire discloses that 36 panel members were examined. Only two persons were excused for cause during the process of selecting 12 jurors and two alternates. The state and defense each interrogated the panelists extensively regarding the homicide's victim's membership in a motorcycle gang called the 'Chosen Few.' The persons excused for cause expressed apprehension about retaliation by the Chosen Few against them or their families if they were members of a jury which acquitted defendant. Most panelists did not share this apprehension. In addition most had been unaffected by pre-trial publicity; few could remember what they may have read or heard about the case." *Des Moines Register v. Osmundson.*

**Vortex Public Figure.** See Pervasive Public Figure.

**Warranty.** A promise by a maker or seller of goods or services guaranteeing asserted standards of quality and performance. Warranties should be specific as to what is covered, who is responsible, what redress is possible for defective merchandise and what the customer must do to get the warranty fulfilled.

**Wheeler-Lea Amendment.** A 1938 amendment to Section 5 of the Federal Trade Commission Act which added to the regulatory power of the FTC. Prior to the amendment, the FTC could act against deceptive advertising only when it was within "unfair methods of competition in commerce." The amendment added "and unfair or deceptive acts or practices in commerce," thereby enabling the FTC to act against misleading advertising regardless whether the advertising adversely affected competition. The amendment enabled the FTC to become a consumer protection agency rather than merely a competition policing agency.

**Widow or Widower (Copyright).** The author's surviving spouse under the law of the author's domicile at the time of his or her death, whether or not the spouse has later remarried.

**Wilmot's Doctrine.** The belief that courts have inherent power to punish for constructive or out-of-court contempt by summary proceeding is traced to a 1765 case in England wherein Justice Wilmot wrote that such power was deeply rooted in common law. But the case at issue was dropped, and Wilmot's opinion was never formally recorded. It was found among his papers and published posthumously. Competent modern authorities find no common law roots for a summary proceeding in constructive contempt. Constructive contempt is now governed by the clear and present danger doctrine and presents little if any threat to media.

**Words of Art.** Words and phrases may have one meaning in literary use and another in their usage in various professions. For example, one of the words used to describe the damage done by libel is "hatred," that is, that the defamation causes a person's friends and neighbors to hate him. But the word is a word of art in libel in that it describes the seriousness of libel but it is not required that people hiss "I hate you" at the defamed person as he passes by or otherwise literally abhor him.

**Work Made for Hire (Copyright).** This is 1. a work prepared by an employee within the scope of his or her employment; or 2. a work specially ordered or commissioned for use as a contribution to a collective work, as part of a motion picture or other audio-visual work, as a translation, as a supplementary work, as a compilation, as an instructional text, as a test, as an answer material for a test, or as an atlas, if the parties expressly agree in a written instrument signed by them that the work shall be considered a work made for hire. In works for hire, the copyright goes to the hirer.

**Work of the U.S. Government (Copyright).** A work prepared by an officer or employee of the U.S. government as part of that person's official duties. Such a work is not copyrightable, but the government is not precluded from receiving and holding copyrights transferred to it by assignment, bequest, or otherwise.

**Writ of Prohibition.** An order from a superior to an inferior court which prohibits the court from going beyond its legitimate authority in some matter. It's considered an extraordinary writ, meaning it applies to circumstances which cannot be handled by ordinary proceedings. The Florida Supreme Court ruled that such a writ was not justified where a reporter challenged a trial judge's decision to exclude the press from a divorce trial since the exclusionary order was not per se beyond the court's authority. "Prohibition is an extraordinary writ, a prerogative writ, extremely narrow in scope and operation, by which a superior court . . . may prevent such inferior court or tribunal from exceeding jurisdiction or usurping jurisdiction over matters not within its jurisdiction." *English v. McCrary.*

# Z

**Zapple Doctrine.** Broadcast time sold or given during a campaign to supporters of a political candidate must be matched by access to comparable time for supporters of opposing candidates. The rule is named after Nicholas Zapple, then a staff assistant to the Senate Subcommittee on Communications, who raised the question in a 1970 letter to the Federal Communications Commission.

**Zone of Privacy.** A phrase used by the U.S. Supreme Court in *Cox Broadcasting Co. v. Cohn* as descriptive of a constitutional right, the limits of which have not yet been defined. The court said: ". . . powerful arguments can be made, and have been made, that however it may be ultimately defined, there *is* a zone of privacy surrounding every individual, a zone within which the state may protect him from intrusion by the press, with all its attendant publicity." In *Cox*, the court found that this zone of privacy did not extend to information taken from court records.

**Zone of Reasonableness** In enforcing equal employment opportunity in licensed media, the FCC uses this phrase as a guide. It involves a "reasonable" relationship between the percentage of women and minorities on the station's staff and their percentage in the area's work force. *Bilingual Bicultural Coalition v. FCC*.

# appendixes

# CASES

Adams v. Frontier Broadcasting, 555 P. 2d 556 (1976)

American Communications Assoc. v. Douds, 339 U.S. 382 (1950)

Ansalmi v. Denver Post, 552 F. 2d 315 (1977)

Associated Press v. NLRB, 301 U.S. 103 (1937)

Associated Press v. United States, 326 U.S. 1 (1945)

Bandelin v. Pietsch, 563 P. 2d 395 (1977)

Banzhaf v. FCC, 405 F. 2d 1082 (1968)

Baker v. Selden, 101 U.S. 99 (1879)

Barber v. Time, 159 S.W. 2d 291 (1948)

Barr v. Mateo, 360 U.S. 564 (1959)

Beauharnais v. Illinois, 343 U.S. 250 (1952)

Bilingual Bicultural Coalition v. FCC, 2 Med. L. Rptr. 1705 (1977)

Branzburg v. Hayes, 408 U.S. 665 (1972)

Bridges v. California, 314 U.S. 252 (1941)

Briscoe v. Reader's Digest, 483 P. 2d 34 (1971)

Brandenburg v. Ohio, 395 U.S. 444 (1969)

Brandon v. Gazette Publishing Co., 352 S.W. 2d 92 (1961)

Burstyn v. Wilson 343 U.S. 495 (1952)

Butler v. Michigan, 352 U.S. 380 (1957)

Callahan v. Westinghouse Broadcasting, 363 N.E. 2d 240 (1977)

Caminetti v. United States, 242 U.S. 468 (1917)

Campbell v. New York Evening Post, 157 N.E. 153 (1927)

Cantrell v. Forest City Publishing, 419 U.S. 245 (1974)

Carlay v. FTC, 153 F. 2d 493 (1946)

Carson v. Allied News Co., 529 F. 2d 206 (1976)

Chaplinsky v. New Hampshire, 315 U.S. 568 (1942)

City of Chicago v. Tribune Co., 139 N.E. 86 (1923)

Citizens Publishing Co. v. United States, 394 U.S. 131 (1969)

Columbia Broadcasting System, Inc. v. Democratic National Committee, 412 U.S. 94 (1973)

Committee on Masonic Homes v. NLRB, 556 F. 2d 214 (1977)

Cox v. Louisiana, 379 U.S. 536 (1965)

Cox Broadcasting Co. v. Cohn, 420 U.S. 469 (1975)

Curtis Publishing Co. v. Butts, 388 U.S. 130 (1967)

Craig v. Harney, 331 U.S. 367 (1947)

Daily Times Democrat v. Graham, 162 So. 2d 474 (1964)

Dennis v. United States, 341 U.S. 494 (1951)

Dietemann v. Time, 449 F. 2d 245 (1971)

Des Moines Register v. Osmundson, 248 N.W. 2d 493 (1976)

Edwards v. National Audubon Society, 556 F. 2d 113 (1977)

English v. McCrary, Jr., 348 So. 2d 293 (1977)

Estes v. Texas, 381 U.S. 532 (1965)

Ex Parte Jackson, 96 U.S. 727 (1877)

FCC v. American Broadcasting Co., 347 U.S. 284 (1954)

Federal Radio Commission v. Nelson Bros., 289 U.S. 266 (1933)

Feiner v. New York, 340 U.S. 315 (1951)

First National Bank of Boston v. Bellotti, 3 Med. L. Rptr. 2105 (1978)

Florida ex rel. Miami Herald v. McIntosh, 340 So. 2d 904 (1977)

Florida Publishing Co. v. Fletcher, 340 So. 2d 914 (1976)

Forcade v. Knight, 416 F. Supp. 1025 (1976)

Freedman v. Maryland, 380 U.S. 51 (1965)

Gannett Co. v. De Pasquale, 401 N.Y.S. 2d 756 (1977)

Garrett v. Estelle, 556 F. 2d 1274 (1977)

Garrison v. Louisiana, 379 U.S. 64 (1964)

Gertz v. Welch, 418 U.S. 323 (1974)

Ginsberg v. New York, 390 U.S. 629 (1968)

Ginzburg v. United States, 383 U.S. 463 (1966)

Gitlow v. New York, 268 U.S. 652 (1925)

Grosjean v. American Press, 297 U.S. 233 (1936)

Hannegan v. Esquire, 327 U.S. 146 (1946)

Harris v. United States, 382 U.S. 162 (1965)

Herald Co. v. McNeal, 553 F. 2d 1125 (1977)

Home Box Office v. FCC, 2 Med. L. Rptr. 1561 (1977)

Houghton v. Payne, 194 U.S. 88 (1904)

Hoover v. Intercity Radio, 286 F. 1003 (1923)

In Re Gault, 387 U.S. 1 (1966)

In Re Oliver, 333 U.S. 257 (1948)

Institute for Scientific Information v. Postal Service, 555 F. 2d 128 (1977)

International News Service v. Associated Press, 248 U.S. 215 (1918)

Jaikens v. Jaikens, 162 N.W. 2d 325 (1968)

Kash Enterprises v. Los Angeles, 138 Cal. Rptr. 53 (1977)

Kimmerle v. New York Evening Journal, 186 N.E. 217 (1933)

Kingsley Pictures v. New York, 360 U.S. 684 (1959)

Kleindienst v. Mandel, 408 U.S. 753 (1972)

Kovacs v. Cooper, 336 U.S. 77 (1949)

KQED and NAACP v. Houchins, 2 Med. L. Rptr. 1115 (1976)

Kunz v. New York, 340 U.S. 290 (1951)

Lamont v. Postmaster General, 381 U.S. 301 (1965)

Lorain Journal v. United States, 342 U.S. 142 (1951)

Los Angeles Free Press v. City of Los Angeles, 88 Cal. Rptr. 605 (1970)

Lovell v. Griffin, 303 U.S. 444 (1938)

Martin Marietta Corp. v. Evening Star Newspaper, 417 F. Supp. 947 (1976)

Miami Herald Publishing Co. v. Tornillo, 418 U.S. 241 (1974)

Midwest Video v. FCC, 46 U.S. Law Week 2477 (1978)

Miller v. California, 413 U.S. 15 (1973)

Mills v. Alabama, 384 U.S. 214 (1966)

Mishkin v. New York, 383 U.S. 502 (1966)

Mt. Mansfield Television v. FCC, 442 F. 2d 470 (1971)

Mutual Film Corp. v. Industrial Commission of Ohio, 236 U.S. 230 (1915)

NAACP v. Alabama, 357 U.S. 449 (1958)

National Broadcasting Co. v. United States, 319 U.S. 190 (1943)

National Citizens Committee for Broadcasting v. FCC, 555 F. 2d 938 (1977)

National Citizens Committee for Broadcasting v. FCC, 3 Med. L. Rptr. 1273 (1977)

Near v. Minnesota, 283 U.S. 697 (1931)

Nebraska Press Assoc. v. Stuart, 427 U.S. 539 (1976)

Neiman Marcus v. Lait, 107 F. Supp. 96 (1952)

New York Times v. Sullivan, 376 U.S. 254 (1964)

New York Times v. United States, 403 U.S. 714 (1971)

Nichols v. Universal Pictures, 45 F. 2d 119 (1930)

Nixon v. United States, 418 U.S. 683 (1974)

Nye v. United States, 313 U.S. 33 (1941)

Office of Communication of United Church of Christ v. FCC, 359 F. 2d 944 (1966)

Oklahoma Publishing Co. v. District Court, 555 P. 2d 1286 (1976)

Pacifica Foundation v. FCC, 2 Med. L. Rptr. 1465 (1977)

Peagler v. Phoenix Newspapers, 560 P. 2d 1216 (1977)

Pearson v. Dodd, 410 F. 2d 701 (1969)

Phillips v. Evening Star Newspaper, 2 Med. L. Rptr. 2201 (1977)

Pittsburgh Press v. Human Relations Commission, 413 U.S. 376 (1973)

Red Lion Broadcasting Co. v. FCC, 395 U.S. 367 (1969)

Regina v. Hicklin, 3 Q.B. 360 (1868)

Rockwell v. Morris, 211 N.Y.S. 2d 25 (1961)

Rosato v. Superior Court of Fresno County, 124 Cal. Rptr. 427 (1975)

Rosenblatt v. Baer, 383 U.S. 75 (1966)

Roth v. United States, 354 U.S. 476 (1957)

Rowan v. Post Office, 397 U.S. 728 (1970)

Sadowski v. Shevin, 351 So. 2d 44 (1976)

Saia v. New York, 334 U.S. 558 (1948)

Sanford v. Boston Herald-Traveler, 61 N.E. 2d 5 (1945)

Schenck v. United States, 249 U.S. 47 (1919)

Schneider v. United States, 308 U.S. 147 (1939)

Scientific Manufacturing v. FTC, 124 F. 2d 640 (1941)

Sheppard v. Maxwell, 384 U.S. 333 (1966)

Shuck v. Carroll Daily Herald, 247 N.W. 813 (1933)

Snowden v. Pearl River Broadcasting, 251 So. 2d 405 (1971)

St. Amant v. Thompson, 390 U.S. 727 (1968)

Stanford Daily v. Zurcher, 550 F. 2d 464 (1977)

State v. Morrill, 16 Ark. 384 (1855)

Talley v. California, 362 U.S. 60 (1960)

Terminiello v. Chicago, 337 U.S. 1 (1949)

Time v. Hill, 385 U.S. 374 (1967)

Time v. Pape, 401 U.S. 279 (1971)

Times Picayune v. United States, 345 U.S. 594 (1953)

Tinker v. Des Moines Independent School District, 393 U.S. 503 (1969)

Toledo Newspaper Co. v. United States, 247 U.S. 402 (1918)

United States v. Associated Press, 52 F. Supp. 362 (1943)

United States v. Cianfrani, 46 U.S. Law Week 2521 (1978)

United States v. Columbia Broadcasting, 47 F. 2d 107 (1974)

United States v. Dickinson, 465 F. 2d 496 (1972)

United States v. Marchetti, 466 F. 2d 1309 (1972)

United States v. Midwest Video Corp., 406 U.S. 609 (1972)

United States v. O'Brien, 391 U.S. 367 (1967)

United States v. Simpson, 561 F. 2d 53 (1977)

United States v. One Book Called Ulysses, 5 F. Supp. 182 (1933)

United States v. Southwestern Cable Co., 392 U.S. 157 (1968)

United States v. Zenith Radio, 12 F. 2d 614 (1926)

Valentine v. Chrestensen, 316 U.S. 52 (1942)

Virginia Board of Pharmacy v. Virginia Citizens Consumer Council, 425 U.S. 748 (1976)

Warner-Lambert v. FTC, 2 Med. L. Rptr. 2303 (1977)

Washington Post v. Keogh, 365 F. 2d 965 (1966)

West Virginia Board of Education v. Barnette, 319 U.S. 624 (1943)

Whitney v. California, 274 U.S. 357 (1927)

Writer's Guild v. FCC, 2 Med. L. Rptr. 1009 (1976)

Young v. American Mini Theaters, 427 U.S. (1976)

Zacchini v. Scripps-Howard, 351 N.E. 2d 454 (1976); 433 U.S. 562 (1977)

Zemel v. Rusk, 381 U.S. 1 (1965)

(Copyright Definitions, Title 17 U.S.C.A. Section 101)

Adams v. Frontier Broadcasting
    Tape Delay System

American Communications Assoc. v. Douds
    Ad Hoc Balancing Test

Ansalmi v. Denver Post
    Long-Arm Statute

Associated Press v. NLRB
    Union Membership

Associated Press v. United States
    Antitrust
    State Action

Bandelin v. Pietsch
    Summary Judgment

Banzhaf v. FCC
    Counter Advertising

Baker v. Selden
    Fair Use

Barber v. Time
    Privacy

Barr v. Mateo
    Privileges—Absolute

Beauharnais v. Illinois
    Libel—Group

Bilingual Bicultural Coalition v. FCC
    Zone of Reasonableness

Branzburg v. Hayes
    Access to Information
    Grand Jury
    Newsman's (Woman's) Privilege

Bridges v. California
    Censorship
    Clear and Present Danger
    Trial by Newspaper

Briscoe v. Reader's Digest
    Privacy

Brandenburg v. Ohio
  Incitement
  Syndicalism Laws

Brandon v. Gazette Publishing Co.
  Consent to Libel

Burstyn v. Wilson
  Motion Pictures

Butler v. Michigan
  Variable Obscenity

Callahan v. Westinghouse Broadcasting
  Clear and Convincing Evidence

Caminetti v. United States
  Statutory Law

Cantrell v. Forest City Publishing
  Respondeat Superior

Campbell v. New York Evening Post
  Pleadings

Carlay v. FTC
  Puffery

Carson v. Allied News Co.
  Term of Art

Chaplinsky v. New Hampshire
  Fighting Words
  Social Value Theory

City of Chicago v. Tribune Co.
  Libel on Government

Citizens Publishing Co. v. United States
  Newspaper Preservation Act

Columbia Broadcasting System, Inc. v. Democratic National
  Committee
    Counter Advertising
    Newsworthiness

Committee on Masonic Homes v. NLRB
  Union Authorization Cards

Cox v. Louisiana
  Symbolic Speech

Houghton v. Payne
    Periodical

Hoover v. Intercity Radio
    Radio Act of 1912, 1927

In Re Gault
    Juvenile Offenders

In Re Oliver
    Public Trial

Institute for Scientific Information v. Postal Service
    Periodical

International News Service v. Associated Press
    Property Right in News
    Publici Juris

Jaikens v. Jaikens
    Contempt—Civil, Criminal

Kash Enterprises v. Los Angeles
    Constitutionally Vague
    Time, Place and Manner

Kimmerle v. New York Evening Journal
    Defamation

Kingsley Pictures v. New York
    Motion Pictures

Kleindienst v. Mandel
    Passport

Kovacs v. Cooper
    Impact Theory
    Loudspeakers

KQED and NAACP v. Houchins
    Access to Information

Kunz v. New York
    Impact Theory

Lamont v. Postmaster General
    Right to Receive Information

Lorain Journal v. United States
    Right to Refuse Advertising

Los Angeles Free Press v. City of Los Angeles
    Press Card

Lovell v. Griffin
    Press

New York Times v. Sullivan
  Appellant-Appelee
  Breathing Space
  Commercial Speech
  Extreme Departure Test
  Landmark Case
  Malice—Actual
  New York Times Rule
  Public Law of Libel
  Self-Censorship

New York Times v. United States
  National Security

Nichols v. Universal Pictures
  Abstractions Test

Nixon v. United States
  Executive Privilege

Nye v. United States
  Contempt—1831 Statute

Office of Communication of United Church of Christ v. FCC
  Standing

Oklahoma Publishing Co. v. District Court
  Juvenile Offenders
  Parens Patriae

Pacifica Foundation v. FCC
  Indecent Language (Broadcasting)

Peagler v. Phoenix Newspapers
  Negligence

Pearson v. Dodd
  Intrusion

Phillips v. Evening Star Newspaper
  Hot Line

Pittsburgh Press v. Human Relations Commission
  A Fortiori

Red Lion Broadcasting Co. v. FCC
  Fairness Doctrine
  Fiduciary
  Impact Theory
  Marketplace of Ideas
  Personal Attacks
  Radio Act of 1912, 1927
  Section 315

Regina v. Hicklin
    Most Susceptible Person Test

Rockwell v. Morris
    Hostile Audience

Rosato v. Superior Court of Fresno County
    Shield Laws

Rosenblatt v. Baer
    Public Official

Roth v. United States
    Absolute Test
    Landmark Case
    Lascivious
    Redeeming Social Importance
    Scienter
    Two-tiered Theory

Rowan v. Post Office
    Pandering Advertising Act

Sadowski v. Shevin
    Political Season

Saia v. New York
    Loudspeakers

Sanford v. Boston Herald-Traveler
    Pleadings

Schenck v. United States
    Clear and Present Danger
    Shouting Fire
    Time of War

Schneider v. United States
    Balancing Test

Scientific Manufacturing v. FTC
    Federal Trade Commission

Sheppard v. Maxwell
    Continuance
    Decision
    Habeas Corpus
    Sua Sponte
    Trial by Newspaper

Shuck v. Carroll Daily Herald
    Public Utility

Snowden v. Pearl River Broadcasting
    Tape Delay System

St. Amant v. Thompson
    Malice—Actual

Stanford Daily v. Zurcher
    Search Warrent

State v. Morrill
    Contempt—1831 Statute

Talley v. California
    Anonymous Expression

Terminiello v. Chicago
    Fighting Words

Time v. Hill
    False Light

Time v. Pape
    Alleged

Times Picayune v. United States
    Tying

Tinker v. Des Moines Independent School District
    Absolute Test
    Material and Substantial Inference

Toledo Newspaper Co. v. United States
    Contempt—1831 Statute
    Reasonable Tendency Doctrine

United States v. Associated Press
    Multitude of Tongues

United States v. Cianfrani
    Public Trial

United States v. Columbia Broadcasting System
    Sketching
    Sub Judice

United States v. Dickinson
    Exhaustion Doctrine

United States v. Marchetti
    Secrecy Agreement

United States v. Midwest Video Corp.
    Ancillary Regulation

United States v. O'Brien
  Incidental Restriction Doctrine
  Symbolic Speech

United States v. One Book Called Ulysses
  Average Person Test

United States v. Simpson
  Noscitur A Sociis

United States v. Southwestern Cable Co.
  CATV

United States v. Zenith Radio
  Radio Act of 1912, 1927

Valentine v. Chrestensen
  Chrestensen Doctrine

Virginia State Board of Pharmacy v. Virginia Citizens Consumers
  Council
  Commercial Speech

Warner-Lambert v. FTC
  Corrective Advertising

Washington Post v. Keogh
  Summary Judgment
  Truth

West Virginia State Board of Education v. Barnette
  Orthodoxy

Whitney v. California
  Advocacy

Writer's Guild v. FCC
  Family Viewing Policy
  State Action

Young v. American Mini Theaters
  Content Neutrality
  Detroit Ordinance
  Incidental Restriction Doctrine

Zacchini v. Scripps-Howard
  Appropriation
  Right of Publicity

Zemel v. Rusk
  Passport

# WORKS

Arthur, William R. and Crosman, Ralph L. *The Law of Newspapers.* New York: McGraw-Hill, 1940.

Brant, Irving. *The Bill of Rights.* New York: New American Library, 1965.

Carmen, Ira H. *Movies, Censorship and the Law.* Ann Arbor, Mich.: The University of Michigan Press, 1966.

Cavallo, Robert M. and Kahan, Stuart. *Photography: What's the Law?* New York: Crown Publishers, Inc., 1976.

Chafee, Zechariah, Jr. *Free Speech in the United States.* Cambridge, Mass.: The Harvard University Press, 1964.

Commission on Freedom of the Press. *A Free and Responsible Press.* Chicago: The University of Chicago Press, 1947.

Devol, Kenneth S. *Mass Media and the Supreme Court.* New York: Hastings House, 1971.

Emerson, Thomas I. *Toward a General Theory of the First Amendment.* New York: Random House, 1963.

Emery, Walter B. *Broadcasting and Government.* East Lansing, Mich.: Michigan State University Press, 1966.

Francois, William E. *Mass Media Law and Regulation.* Columbus, Ohio: Grid, Inc., 1975.

Franklin, Marc A. *The First Amendment and the Fourth Estate.* Mineola, N.Y.: The Foundation Press, 1977.

Gillmor, Donald M. and Barron, Jerome A. *Mass Communication Law.* Second Edition. St. Paul: West Publishing Co., 1974.

Goldfarb, Ronald L. *The Contempt Power.* New York: Columbia University Press, 1963.

Gora, Joel M. *The Rights of Reporters.* New York: Avon Books, 1974.

Hachten, William A. *The Supreme Court on Freedom of the Press.* Ames, Iowa: The Iowa State University Press, 1968.

Haiman, Franklyn. *Freedom of Speech: Issues and Cases.* New York: Random House, 1965.

Hale, William G. *The Law of the Press.* St. Paul: West Publishing Co., 1948.

Hanson, Arthur B. *Libel and Related Torts*. New York: The American Newspaper Publishers Association Foundation, 1969; Supplements No. 1, 1970: No. 2, 1974; No. 3, 1976.

Head, Sydney W. *Broadcasting in America*. Cambridge, Mass.: The Riverside Press, 1956.

Hocking, William Ernest. *Freedom of the Press*. Chicago: The University of Chicago Press, 1947.

Jones, Robert W. *The Law of Journalism*. Washington: Washington Law Book Co., 1940.

Kronhausen, Drs. Eberhard and Phyllis. *Pornography and the Law*. New York: Ballantine Books, 1959.

Lawhorne, Clifton O. *Defamation and Public Officials: The Evolving Law of Libel*. Carbondale, Ill.: Southern Illinois University Press, 1971.

Levy, Leonard W. *Freedom of Speech and Press in Early American History: Legacy of Suppression*. New York: Harper Torchbooks, 1963.

Nelson, Harold L. and Teeter, Dwight L. Jr. *Law of Mass Communications*. Second Edition. Mineola, N.Y.: The Foundation Press, 1973.

Pember, Don R. *Mass Media Law*. Dubuque, Iowa: William C. Brown Co. Publishers, 1977.

Phelps, Robert H. and Hamilton, E. Douglas. *Libel: Rights, Risks, Responsibilities*. New York: The Macmillan Co., 1966.

Prosser, William L. *Law of Torts*. Fourth Edition. St. Paul: West Publishing Co., 1971.

*Report of the Commission on Obscenity and Pornography*. New York: Bantam Books, 1970.

Schmidt, Benno C. Jr. *Freedom of the Press vs. Public Access*. New York: Praeger Publishers, 1976.

Siebert, Frederick S. *The Rights and Privileges of the Press*. New York: D. Appleton-Century Co., 1934, and *Freedom of the Press in England, 1496-1776*. Urbana, Ill.: The University of Illinois Press, 1965.

Simon, Morton J. *Public Relations Law*. New York: Appleton-Century -Crofts, 1969.

Swindler, William F. *Problems of Law in Journalism*. New York: The Macmillan Co., 1955.

Zuckman, Harvey L. and Gaynes, Martin J. *Mass Communications Law in a Nutshell*. St. Paul: West Publishing Co., 1977.

# ACKNOWLEDGEMENTS

The author gratefully acknowledges the help of Mary Perpich Casteel, a graduate student at MSU, who got this volume started; Mary Hamilton, an instructor of journalism, The Pennsylvania State University, who tolerated conversations about it; David B. Reddick, doctoral student at MSU who steered its final days; Nina Burton, then of our journalism office staff, a versatile helper; and four readers who critically read it and suggested many worthwhile changes— Roger Lane, executive assistant, Michigan Supreme Court; Kay Lockridge, Women in Communications, New York; Dr. Thomas A. Muth, associate professor, Telecommunications, MSU; Stephen C. Bransdorfer, of Miller, Johnson, Snell & Cummiskey, Grand Rapids, and former president, State Bar of Michigan. The author dedicates the book to Fran, Michael, Denise, Mark and Elizabeth.

## ABOUT THE AUTHOR

John Murray, a specialist in the First Amendment, is a
professor of Journalism at Michigan State University and Director
of its Journalism/Law Institute.  Prior to joining the MSU facult
his professional experience included daily and weekly newspaper
reporting, magazine writing and editing, government and political
public relations.  He is a former chairman of the Grievance Board
of the State Bar of Michigan, the only layman to hold that title.
Past or current professional associations include Sigma Delta Chi
The Society of Professional Journalists; the Public Relations
Society of America, Accredited; the National Council of Editorial
Writers, and the Association for Education in Journalism.